COMMON CORE

LANGUAGE ARTS & LITERACY

Activities that Captivate, Motivate & Reinforce

Grade 4

by Marjorie Frank

Incentive Publications
World Book, Inc.
a Scott Fetzer company

Illustrated by Kathleen Bullock
Cover by Penny Laporte
Edited by Joy MacKenzie

ISBN 978-0-86530-742-1

World Book, Inc.
233 North Michigan Avenue
Suite 2000
Chicago, Illinois, 60601 U.S.A.

For information about other World Book publications, visit our website at **www.worldbook.com** or call **1-800-967-5325.**

Printed in the United States by Sheridan Books, Inc.
Chelsea, Michigan
1st Printing May 2013

CONTENTS

Reading—Foundational Skills

Writing

Language

Assessment & Answer Keys

Great Support for Common Core Standards!

Invite your students to join in on mysteries and adventures with colorful characters! They will delight in the high-appeal topics and engaging visuals. They can

. . . sit ringside at a bullfight or a slug race,
. . . take a ride on a stomach-flipping roller coaster,
. . . drop in on a costume ball at Versailles Palace,
. . . find out how to make a mummy,
. . . search for the Loch Ness Monster,
. . . catch sight of a leprechaun or a mermaid,
. . . join a space mission or catch a wily art thief,
. . . learn how to treat alligator bites,
. . . watch the feats of a famous fictitious cowboy,
. . . and tackle many other engaging ventures.

And while they engage in these ventures, they will be moving toward competence with critical language skills and standards that they need for success in the real world.

How to Use this Book

- The pages are tools to support your teaching of the concepts, processes, and skills outlined in the Common Core State Standards. This is not a curriculum; it is a collection of engaging experiences for you to use as you work with your children or students.
- Use any given page to introduce, explain, teach, practice, extend, assess, provide independent work for, start a discussion about, or get students collaborating on a skill or concept.
- Use any page in a large group or small group setting to deepen understandings and expand knowledge or skills.
- Pages are not meant to be used solely as independent work. Do them together, or always review and discuss the work together.
- Each activity is focused on a particular standard or cluster of standards, but most make use of or can be expanded to strengthen other standards as well.
- The book is organized according to the Common Core language strands. Use the tables on pages 9 to 20 and the label on the bottom corner to identify the cluster of standards supported by each page.
- Use the labels on the Contents pages to see specific standards for each page.
- To further mastery of Common Core State Standards, use the suggestions on the next page (page 8).

About Common Core Language Arts & Literacy Standards

The Common Core State Language Arts & Literacy Standards seek to build strong content knowledge across a wide range of subject areas. They are also designed to develop capabilities for thoughtful use of technology and digital media; for finding, applying, and evaluating evidence; for working and thinking independently; and for deepening reasoning and understanding. To best help students gain and master these robust standards for reading, writing, speaking, listening, and language . . .

1. Know the standards well. Keep them in front of you. Understand for yourself the big picture of what the standards seek to do. (See www.corestandards.org.)

2. Work to apply, expand, and deepen student skills. With activities in this book (or any learning activities), plan to include
   . . . interaction with peers in pairs, small groups, and large groups.
   . . . plenty of discussion and integration of language content.
   . . . emphasis on asking questions, analyzing, careful reading and listening, finding evidence, and reasoning.
   . . . lots of observation, meaningful feedback, follow-up, and reflection.

3. Ask questions that advance reasoning, discernment, relevance, and real-life connection:

   - *Why? What does this mean?*
   - *How do you know?*
   - *What led you to this conclusion?*
   - *Where did you find this?*
   - *What else do you know (or need to know)?*
   - *What is the evidence?*
   - *Where else could you look?*
   - *How is _____ like (or unlike) _____?*
   - *What would another viewpoint look like?*
   - *Why do you think that?*
   - *What is the purpose?*
   - *What belief does the author have?*
   - *Do you agree? Why or why not?*
   - *How does this part affect that part?*
   - *Where have you seen something like this before?*
   - *How are the words used?*
   - *What are the parts? How do they work together?*
   - *How does the text confirm your ideas?*
   - *How would this vary for a different purpose, place, person, or situation?*
   - *How does the idea of the text (or speech or argument) build?*
   - *How is this idea affected by the ideas that came before it?*
   - *How could you write (or say) this to give _____ effect?*
   - *What is the effect of using this word (or phrase, or idea, or structure)?*
   - *How is this affected by the writer's (or speaker's) perspective or culture?*
   - *So what? (What difference does this information, or perspective, or discovery make?)*

Grade 4 Common Core State Standards for Language Arts & Literacy

College and Career Readiness Anchor Standards (CCRs) for Reading, Grades K–5

St. #	Standard	Pages that Support
	Key Ideas and Details	
1	Read closely to determine what the text says explicitly and to make logical inferences from it; cite specific textual evidence when writing or speaking to support conclusions drawn from the text.	26, 27, 28, 29, 30, 31, 32, 33, 34, 35, 36, 37, 38, 39, 40, 41, 42, 43, 44, 46, 47, 48, 49, 50, 51, 52, 53, 54, 58, 59, 63, 64, 65, 67, 68
2	Determine central ideas or themes of a text and analyze their development; summarize the key supporting details and ideas.	30, 31, 32, 33, 52, 53, 54, 67, 68
3	Analyze how and why individuals, events, and ideas develop and interact over the course of a text.	34, 35, 36, 50, 51, 67, 68
	Craft and Structure	
4	Interpret words and phrases as they are used in a text, including determining technical, connotative, and figurative meanings, and analyze how specific word choices shape meaning or tone.	22, 23, 24, 25, 55, 56
5	Analyze the structure of texts, including how specific sentences, paragraphs, and larger portions of the text (e.g., a section, chapter, scene, or stanza) relate to each other and the whole.	30, 37, 42, 43, 44, 57, 60
6	Assess how point of view or purpose shapes the content and style of a text.	38, 39, 58, 59
	Integration of Knowledge and Ideas	
7	Integrate and evaluate content presented in diverse media and formats, including visually and quantitatively, as well as in words.	35, 36, 40, 41, 48, 49, 50, 51, 55, 57, 60, 61, 62, 63, 66
8	Delineate and evaluate the argument and specific claims in a text, including the validity of the reasoning as well as the relevance and sufficiency of the evidence.	47, 48, 64, 65
9	Analyze how two or more texts address similar themes or topics in order to build knowledge or to compare the approaches the authors take.	76, 78
	Range of Reading and Level of Text Complexity	
10	Read and comprehend complex literary and informational texts independently and proficiently.	22–44, 46–78

Reading Standards for Literature, Grade 4

St. #	Standard	Pages that Support
	Key Ideas and Details	
1	Refer to details and examples in a text when explaining what the text says explicitly and when drawing inferences from the text.	26, 27, 28, 29, 30, 31, 32, 33, 34, 35, 36, 37, 38, 39, 40, 41, 42, 43, 44
2	Determine a theme of a story, drama, or poem from details in the text; summarize the text.	30, 31, 32, 33
3	Describe in depth a character, setting, or event in a story or drama, drawing on specific details in the text (e.g., a character's thoughts, words, or actions).	34, 35, 36
	Craft and Structure	
4	Determine the meaning of words and phrases as they are used in a text, including those that allude to significant characters found in mythology (e.g., Herculean).	22, 23, 24, 25
5	Explain major differences between poems, drama, and prose, and refer to the structural elements of poems (e.g., verse, rhythm, meter) and drama (e.g., casts of characters, settings, descriptions, dialogue, stage directions) when writing or speaking about a text.	30, 37, 42, 43, 44
6	Compare and contrast the point of view from which different stories are narrated, including the difference between first- and third-person narrations.	38, 39
	Integration of Knowledge and Ideas	
7	Make connections between the text of a story or drama and a visual or oral presentation of the text, identifying where each version reflects specific descriptions and directions in the text.	35, 36, 40, 41
8	(not applicable to literature)	
9	Compare and contrast the treatment of similar themes and topics (e.g., opposition of good and evil) and patterns of events (e.g., the quest) in stories, myths, and traditional literature from different cultures.	*Not covered here*
	Range of Reading and Level of Text Complexity	
10	By the end of the year, read and comprehend literature, including stories, dramas, and poetry, in the grades 4–5 text complexity band independently and proficiently, with scaffolding as needed at the high end of the range.	22, 23, 24, 25, 26, 27, 28, 29, 30, 31, 32, 33, 34, 35, 36, 37, 38, 39, 40, 41, 42, 43, 44

Reading Standards for Informational Text, Grade 4

St. #	Standard	Pages that Support
	Key Ideas and Details	
1	Refer to details and examples in a text when explaining what the text says explicitly and when drawing inferences from the text.	46, 47, 48, 49, 50, 51, 52, 53, 54, 58, 59, 63, 64, 65, 67, 68
2	Determine the main idea of a text and explain how it is supported by key details; summarize the text.	52, 53, 54, 67, 68
3	Explain events, procedures, ideas, or concepts in a historical, scientific, or technical text, including what happened and why, based on specific information in the text.	50, 51, 67, 68
	Craft and Structure	
4	Determine the meaning of general academic and domain-specific words or phrases in a text relevant to a *grade 4 topic or subject area.*	55, 56
5	Describe the overall structure (e.g., chronology, comparison, cause/effect, and problem/solution) of events, ideas, concepts, or information in a text or part of a text.	57, 60
6	Compare and contrast a firsthand and secondhand account of the same event or topic; describe the differences in focus and the information provided.	58, 59
	Integration of Knowledge and Ideas	
7	Interpret information presented visually, orally, or quantitatively (e.g., in charts, graphs, diagrams, time lines, animations, or interactive elements on Web pages) and explain how the information contributes to an understanding of the text in which it appears.	35, 36, 48, 49, 50, 51, 55, 57, 60, 61, 62, 63, 66
8	Explain how an author uses reasons and evidence to support particular points in a text.	47, 48, 64, 65
9	Integrate information from two texts on the same topic in order to write or speak about the subject knowledgeably.	67, 68
	Range of Reading and Level of Text Complexity	
10	By the end of year, read and comprehend informational texts, including history/social studies, science, and technical texts, in the grades 4–5 text complexity band proficiently, with scaffolding as needed at the high end of the range.	46, 47, 48, 49, 50, 51, 52, 53, 54, 55, 56, 57, 58, 59, 60, 61, 62, 63, 64, 65, 66, 67, 68

Reading Standards: Foundational Skills for Grade 4

St. #	Standard	Pages that Support
	Phonics and Word Recognition	
1	(Kindergarten and Grade 1 Standard)	
2	(Kindergarten and Grade 1 Standard)	
3	Know and apply grade-level phonics and word analysis skills in decoding words.	
3a	Use combined knowledge of all letter-sound correspondences, syllabication patterns, and morphology (e.g., roots and affixes) to read accurately unfamiliar multisyllabic words in context and out of context.	23, 24, 25, 70, 71, 72, 73, 74, 75, 76, 77, 78
	Fluency	
4	Read with sufficient accuracy and fluency to support comprehension.	*See below.*
4a	Read on-level text with purpose and understanding.	*See below.*
4b	Read on-level prose and poetry orally with accuracy, appropriate rate, and expression on successive readings.	*See below.*
4c	Use context to confirm or self-correct word recognition and understanding, rereading as necessary.	*See below.*

Standard 4: *To nourish and assess fluency, it is necessary to listen to students read aloud and/or discuss with them the texts they read. Many pages in this book include stories, questions, or other texts that can be used to support or develop fluency and its connection to comprehension. Pages such as these can be used for this purpose: 22, 23, 24, 25, 26, 27, 31, 32, 33, 34,37, 38, 39, 40, 44, 47, 50, 51, 52 53, 54, 55, 58, 59, 61, 64, 65, 66, 67, 68.*

College and Career Readiness Anchor Standards (CCRs) for Writing, Grades K-5

St. #	Standard	Pages that Support
	Text Types and Purposes	
1	Write arguments to support claims in an analysis of substantive topics or texts, using valid reasoning and relevant and sufficient evidence.	80, 81, 82
2	Write informative/explanatory texts to examine and convey complex ideas and information clearly and accurately through the effective selection, organization, and analysis of content.	83, 84
3	Write narratives to develop real or imagined experiences or events using effective technique, well-chosen details, and well-structured event sequences.	85, 86, 87
	Production and Distribution of Writing	
4	Produce clear and coherent writing in which the development, organization, and style are appropriate to task, purpose, and audience.	80, 81, 82, 83, 84, 85, 86, 87, 88, 89, 90, 91, 92, 93, 94, 95, 96
5	Develop and strengthen writing as needed by planning, revising, editing, rewriting, or trying a new approach.	88, 89, 90, 91, 92, 93, 94, 95, 96
6	Use technology, including the Internet, to produce and publish writing and to interact and collaborate with others.	*Not covered here*
	Research to Build and Present Knowledge	
7	Conduct short as well as more sustained research projects based on focused questions, demonstrating understanding of the subject under investigation.	93, 94
8	Gather relevant information from multiple print and digital sources, assess the credibility and accuracy of each source, and integrate the information while avoiding plagiarism.	93, 94
9	Draw evidence from literary or informational texts to support analysis, reflection, and research.	95, 96
	Range of Writing	
10	Write routinely over extended time frames (time for research, reflection, and revision) and shorter time frames (a single sitting or a day or two) for a range of tasks, purposes, and audiences.	80, 81, 82, 83, 84, 85, 86, 87, 88, 89, 90, 91, 92, 93, 94, 95, 96

Writing Standards for Grade 4

St. #	Standard	Pages that Support
	Text Types and Purposes	
1	Write opinion pieces on topics or texts, supporting a point of view with reasons and information.	
1a	Introduce a topic or text clearly, state an opinion, and create an organizational structure in which related ideas are grouped to support the writer's purpose.	80, 81, 82
1b	Provide reasons that are supported by facts and details.	80, 81, 82
1c	Link opinion and reasons using words and phrases (e.g., *for instance, in order to, in addition*).	80, 81, 82
1d	Provide a concluding statement or section related to the opinion presented.	80, 81, 82
2	Write informative/explanatory texts to examine a topic and convey ideas and information clearly.	
2a	Introduce a topic clearly and group related information in paragraphs and sections; include formatting (e.g., headings), illustrations, and multimedia when useful to aiding comprehension.	83, 84
2b	Develop the topic with facts, definitions, concrete details, quotations, or other information and examples related to the topic.	83, 84
2c	Link ideas within categories of information using words and phrases (e.g., *another, for example, also, because*).	83, 83
2d	Use precise language and domain-specific vocabulary to inform about or explain the topic.	83, 84
2e	Provide a concluding statement or section related to the information or explanation presented.	83, 84
3	Write narratives to develop real or imagined experiences or events using effective technique, descriptive details, and clear event sequences.	
3a	Orient the reader by establishing a situation and introducing a narrator and/or characters; organize an event sequence that unfolds naturally.	85, 86, 87
3b	Use dialogue and description to develop experiences and events or show the responses of characters to situations.	85, 86, 87
3c	Use a variety of transitional words and phrases to manage the sequence of events.	85, 86, 87
3d	Use concrete words and phrases and sensory details to convey experiences and events precisely.	85, 86, 87
3e	Provide a conclusion that follows from the narrated experiences or events.	85, 86, 87

Writing standards continue on next page.

Writing Standards for Grade 4, continued

St. #	Standard	Pages that Support
	Production and Distribution of Writing	
4	Produce clear and coherent writing in which the development and organization are appropriate to task, purpose, and audience. (Grade-specific expectations for writing types are defined in standards 1–3 above.)	80, 81, 82, 83, 84, 85, 86, 87, 88, 89, 90, 91, 92, 93, 94, 95, 96
5	With guidance and support from peers and adults, develop and strengthen writing as needed by planning, revising, and editing.	80, 81, 82, 83, 84, 85, 86, 87, 88, 89, 90, 91, 92, 93, 94, 95, 96
6	With some guidance and support from adults, use technology, including the Internet, to produce and publish writing as well as to interact and collaborate with others; demonstrate sufficient command of keyboarding skills to type a minimum of one page in a single sitting.	*See below.*
	Research to Build and Present Knowledge	
7	Conduct short research projects that build knowledge through investigation of different aspects of a topic.	93, 94
8	Recall relevant information from experiences or gather relevant information from print and digital sources; take notes and categorize information, and provide a list of sources.	93, 94
9	Draw evidence from literary or informational texts to support analysis, reflection, and research.	
9a	Apply *grade 4 Reading standards* to literature (e.g., "Describe in depth a character, setting, or event in a story or drama, drawing on specific details in the text (e.g., a character's thoughts, words, or actions).").	95
9b	Apply *grade 4 Reading standards* to informational texts (e.g., "Explain how an author uses reasons and evidence to support particular points in a text").	96
	Range of Writing	
10	Write routinely over extended time frames (time for research, reflection, and revision) and shorter time frames (a single sitting or a day or two) for a range of discipline-specific tasks, purposes, and audiences.	80, 81, 82, 83, 84, 85, 86, 87, 88, 89, 90, 91, 92, 93, 94, 95, 96

Standard 6: *Use technology as a part of your approach for any of the activities in this writing section. Students can create, dictate, photograph, scan, enhance with art or color, or share any of the products they create as a part of these pages.*

College and Career Readiness Anchor Standards (CCRs) for Speaking & Listening, Grades K–5

St. #	Standard
	Comprehension and Collaboration
1	Prepare for and participate effectively in a range of conversations and collaborations with diverse partners, building on others' ideas and expressing their own clearly and persuasively.
2	Integrate and evaluate information presented in diverse media and formats, including visually, quantitatively, and orally.
3	Evaluate a speaker's point of view, reasoning, and use of evidence and rhetoric.
	Presentation of Knowledge and Ideas
4	Present information, findings, and supporting evidence such that listeners can follow the line of reasoning and the organization, development, and style are appropriate to task, purpose, and audience.
5	Make strategic use of digital media and visual displays of data to express information and enhance understanding of presentations.
6	Adapt speech to a variety of contexts and communicative tasks, demonstrating command of formal English when indicated or appropriate.

Speaking and Listening Standards: *The speaking and listening standards are not specifically addressed in this book. However, most pages can be used for conversation and collaboration. Teachers and parents are encouraged to use the activities in a sharing and discussion format. Many of the pages include visual information that students can include in the integration and evaluation of information.*

In addition, most of the texts and activities can be adapted to listening activities or can be used to support the listening and speaking standards.

Speaking and Listening Standards for Grade 4

St. #	Standard	Pages that Support
	Comprehension and Collaboration	
1	Engage effectively in a range of collaborative discussions (one-on-one, in groups, and teacher-led) with diverse partners on *grade 4 topics and texts*, building on others' ideas and expressing their own clearly.	
1a	Come to discussions prepared, having read or studied required material; explicitly draw on that preparation and other information known about the topic to explore ideas under discussion.	
1b	Follow agreed-upon rules for discussions and carry out assigned roles.	
1c	Pose and respond to specific questions to clarify or follow up on information, and make comments that contribute to the discussion and link to the remarks of others.	
1d	Review the key ideas expressed and explain their own ideas and understanding in light of the discussion.	
2	Paraphrase portions of a text read aloud or information presented in diverse media and formats, including visually, quantitatively, and orally.	
3	Identify the reasons and evidence a speaker provides to support particular points.	
	Presentation of Knowledge and Ideas	
4	Report on a topic or text, tell a story, or recount an experience in an organized manner, using appropriate facts and relevant, descriptive details to support main ideas or themes; speak clearly at an understandable pace.	
5	Add audio recordings and visual displays to presentations when appropriate to enhance the development of main ideas or themes.	
6	Differentiate between contexts that call for formal English (e.g., presenting ideas) and situations where informal discourse is appropriate (e.g., small-group discussion); use formal English when appropriate to task and situation.	

Speaking and Listening Standards: *The speaking and listening standards are not specifically addressed in this book. However, most pages can be used for conversation and collaboration. Teachers and parents are encouraged to use the activities in a sharing and discussion format. Many of the pages include visual information that students can include in the integration and evaluation of information.*

In addition, most of the texts and activities can be adapted to listening activities or can be used to support the listening and speaking standards.

College and Career Readiness Anchor Standards (CCRs) for Language, Grades K-5

St. #	Standard	Pages that Support
	Conventions of Standard English	
1	Demonstrate command of the conventions of standard English grammar and usage when writing or speaking.	98, 99, 100, 101, 102, 103, 104
2	Demonstrate command of the conventions of standard English capitalization, punctuation, and spelling when writing.	105, 106, 107, 108, 109, 110, 111
	Knowledge of Language	
3	Apply knowledge of language to understand how language functions in different contexts, to make effective choices for meaning or style, and to comprehend more fully when reading or listening.	112, 113, 114
	Vocabulary Acquisition and Use	
4	Determine or clarify the meaning of unknown and multiple-meaning words and phrases by using context clues, analyzing meaningful word parts, and consulting general and specialized reference materials, as appropriate.	115, 116, 117, 118, 119, 120, 121, 122, 123, 124, 125, 126
5	Demonstrate understanding of figurative language, word relationships, and nuances in word meanings.	121, 122, 123
6	Acquire and use accurately a range of general academic and domain-specific words and phrases sufficient for reading, writing, speaking, and listening at the college and career readiness level; demonstrate independence in gathering vocabulary knowledge when encountering an unknown term important to comprehension or expression.	98, 99, 100, 101, 102, 103, 104, 105, 106, 107, 108, 109, 110, 111, 112, 113, 114, 115, 116, 117, 118, 119, 120, 121, 122, 123, 124, 125, 126

Language Standards for Grade 4

St. #	Standard	Pages that Support
	Conventions of Standard English	
1	Demonstrate command of the conventions of standard English grammar and usage when writing or speaking.	
1a	Use relative pronouns *(who, whose, whom, which, that)* and relative adverbs *(where, when, why)*.	98
1b	Form and use the progressive (e.g., *I was walking; I am walking; I will be walking*) verb tenses.	99
1c	Use modal auxiliaries (e.g., *can, may, must*) to convey various conditions.	100
1d	Order adjectives within sentences according to conventional patterns (e.g., *a small red bag* rather than *a red small bag*).	101
1e	Form and use prepositional phrases.	102
1f	Produce complete sentences, recognizing and correcting inappropriate fragments and run-ons.*	103
1g	Correctly use frequently confused words (e.g., *to, too, two; there, their*).*	104
2	Demonstrate command of the conventions of standard English capitalization, punctuation, and spelling when writing.	
2a	Use correct capitalization.	105
2b	Use commas and quotation marks to mark direct speech and quotations from a text.	106, 107
2c	Use a comma before a coordinating conjunction in a compound sentence.	106
2d	Spell grade-appropriate words correctly, consulting references as needed.	108, 109, 110, 111

Language standards continue on next page.

Language Standards for Grade 4, continued

St. #	Standard	Pages that Support
	Knowledge of Language	
3	Use knowledge of language and its conventions when writing, speaking, reading, or listening.	
3a	Choose words and phrases to convey ideas precisely.*	112
3b	Choose punctuation for effect.*	113
3c	Differentiate between contexts that call for formal English (e.g., presenting ideas) and situations where informal discourse is appropriate (e.g., small-group discussion).	114
	Vocabulary Acquisition and Use	
4	Determine or clarify the meaning of unknown and multiple-meaning words and phrases based on *grade 4 reading and content*, choosing flexibly from a range of strategies.	
4a	Use context (e.g., definitions, examples, or restatements in text) as a clue to the meaning of a word or phrase.	115, 116, 117
4b	Use common, grade-appropriate Greek and Latin affixes and roots as clues to the meaning of a word (e.g., *telegraph, photograph, autograph*).	118, 119
4c	Consult reference materials (e.g., dictionaries, glossaries, thesauruses), both print and digital, to find the pronunciation and determine or clarify the precise meaning of key words and phrases.	120, 126
5	Demonstrate understanding of figurative language, word relationships, and nuances in word meanings.	
5a	Explain the meaning of simple similes and metaphors (e.g., *as pretty as a picture*) in context.	121
5b	Recognize and explain the meaning of common idioms, adages, and proverbs.	122, 123
5c	Demonstrate understanding of words by relating them to their opposites (antonyms) and to words with similar but not identical meanings (synonyms).	124, 125
6	Acquire and use accurately grade-appropriate general academic and domain-specific words and phrases, including those that signal precise actions, emotions, or states of being (e.g., quizzed, whined, stammered) and that are basic to a particular topic (e.g., *wildlife, conservation*, and *endangered* when discussing animal preservation).	126

READING

LITERATURE

Grade 4

ADVENTURES UNLIMITED

Let us take you on the adventure of your dreams. ***Adventures Unlimited*** is the place to shop for any kind of travel! We'll take you to real or fantasy locations in the past, present, or future. Choose your adventure—and start packing!

Find a word on one of the posters that matches each direction below.
Look on both pages (pages 22 and 23).

Find a word that is a synonym for . . .

1. adventure ____________________
2. sail ____________________
3. tricks ____________________
4. socialize ____________________
5. examine ____________________
6. try ____________________
7. travel ____________________

Find two synonyms for *search*.

8. ____________________

   ____

Find a word or phrase that means . . .

9. make-believe ____________________
10. grand ____________________
11. having to do with food ____________________
12. climb ____________________

Use with page 23.

Name

Find a word on one of the posters that matches each direction below.
Look on both pages (pages 22 and 23).

Write a word that is an antonym for . . .

13. safe ________________
14. real ________________
15. modern ________________
16. pleasant ________________
17. small ________________
18. plain & simple ________________
19. believable ________________
20. past ________________

Write a word that is a synonym for . . .

21. hard to catch ________________
22. famous ________________
23. wreck ________________
24. a good price ________________
25. hire ________________
26. a look ________________
27. far away ________________
28. scariest ________________

Use with page 22.

Name ________________

EXPLORE A DEEP CAVE

ADVENTURE #1 Explore the Réseau Jean Bernard Cave, the deepest cave in the world. Bring a hard hat, wear a raincoat, and don't forget the lights!

Find each of the words 1 to 12 in one of the talk balloons. Write what the word means in that sentence.

1. ludicrous ____________________
2. elated ____________________
3. cavern ____________________
4. penetrated ____________________
5. rue ____________________
6. sodden ____________________

7. precarious ____________________
8. hiatus ____________________
9. thwart ____________________
10. carping ____________________
11. disquieted ____________________
12. sinister ____________________

Name

HEAD FOR THE SWAMP

ADVENTURE #2 Venture into the largest swamp in the world—the deep, damp Everglades. Take a swamp boat up the river to see the swamp creatures. If you're ready, we'll give you an alligator-wrestling lesson, too! You'll need a good dose of courage to try this! if you run into trouble, maybe the cures below will help you.

PREVENTING ALLIGATOR BITES

Endeavor to avoid alligator bites at all costs. **Appease** the alligator with the offer of a bag ofrippled potato chips before you start the wrestling match. As a **precautionary** measure, get yourself an alligator-proof suit that is too thick for alligator teeth to **penetrate**. Of course, the **surefire** way to avoid bites is to avoid the alligator!

HOW TO HEAL ALLIGATOR BITES

If an alligator bites you, mix the juice of 12 tomatoes with cooked oatmeal. Squeeze in 7 drops of root beer. Spread this over the **affected** area right away. Then cover the area with warm banana peels and wrap **securely** with plastic wrap. After just an hour, the bite will be **substantially** on its way to healing.

CURE for WARTS

If you end up with warts after an **encounter** with an alligator, you'll be in need of this potion. Pick 3 fresh cabbages. Slice them and drop them in a blender with 2 cups of chocolate milk. Sprinkle in a handful of **tangy** chili powder. Add a **dollop** of mustard and a tablespoon of vinegar to the mixture and blend for 2 minutes at high speed. Drink this at bedtime and sleep for 12 hours. When you awake, the warts will be gone.

CURE for a HEADACHE

It's not uncommon to have a **throbbing** headache after a good wrestling match. The best cure is a good old-fashioned onion wrap. Boil 20 onions in 2 quarts of water for an hour. Add $\frac{1}{2}$ cup of molasses. Soak some old rags in the liquid for several minutes. When they are **saturated**, squeeze out the juice and **envelop** your head with the rags. Sit very still in a dark room, and your headache will **vanish** for sure in 15 minutes.

Match the words from the cures with their correct meanings. Use the context to help you.

___	1. endeavor	a. considerably
___	2. appease	b. pounding
___	2. precautionary	c. disappear
___	4. penetrate	d. try
___	5. surefire	e. spicy
___	6. affected	f. soaked
___	7. securely	g. preventive
___	8. substantially	h. enter
___	9. encounter	i. satisfy
___	10. tangy	j. wrap
___	11. dollop	k. large drop
___	12. throbbing	l. tightly
___	13. saturated	m. foolproof
___	14. envelop	n. hurt
___	15. vanish	o. meeting

Name

CATCH A LEPRECHAUN

ADVENTURE #3 Travel with us to the land of magic. Visit Ireland and hunt for those friendly little elves called **leprechauns**. Catch one (if you can)! Maybe you'll find a pot of gold while you're searching!

With magic you can soar in the clouds with the angels. You can say hello to the fairies, fly on winged unicorns` backs, go to the Amazon Jungle and play with boas and black panthers. Be a wizard, a super hero, a monster, and almost anything! You can smell the prehistoric air, create a time machine and go to the future. Build a giant hunk of metal and create a star-ship. Be the first boy or girl to dig to the pit of the Earth. You can pull a bunny out of your hat. Glide from the stars, and slide down bright, colorful rainbows. Wherever you are, whatever time it is, you can find magic in your heart and you can be anything, and do anything you may want to do!

Paul Ireland, Gr. 4

Use the passage on the mushroom to answer the questions.

1. What does the writing say you can do with magic? Write at least four things.

____

____

____

____

____

____

____

____

2. What is the theme of the writing on the mushroom? ____________________
What helped you identify the theme?

____

____

____

____

____

____

____

Name ______________________________________

Key Ideas, Details

CATCH SIGHT OF A MERMAID

ADVENTURE #4 Wouldn't you like to find a mermaid? Join the hunt! Keep your eyes open, and you might catch a glimpse of these fantastic creatures!

Read Maria's diary about the Mermaid Hunt. Write the main idea for each diary entry. Be ready to explain how you decided on the main idea.

Thursday, May 18

Dear Diary,
Today I joined the crew of the submarine named **Explorer.** We are going on a hunt for mermaids. I have wanted to do this all my life. I am so excited! I hope I see one!
Maria

The main idea is______________________

____

____

Saturday, May 20

Dear Diary,
I've been learning about the history of mermaids today. Irish legends say that mermaids were women who did not follow the religion of their day in Ireland. Because of this, they were banished from the earth by St. Patrick. The only place they had to live was in the sea.
Maria

The main idea is______________________

____

____

____

Tuesday, May 22

Dear Diary,
Along with their belief in mermaids, many people in Ireland and Scotland believe in sea serpents. There are frequent reports of people sighting them. These are huge sea snakes that are about 300 feet long. Stories of the Scottish Loch Ness monster and the kraken of Scandinavia have been told for years. I'm hoping to see a sea serpent, too!
Maria

The main idea is______________________

____

____

Friday, May 25

Dear Diary,
How thrilling! I am just sure I saw a mermaid today. She had the head and body of a woman. Below the waist, the creature was a fish with scales and a long tail. Really! I did see one swimming off the side of the boat!
Maria

The main idea is______________________

____

____

Name ______________________________

ROCK INTO THE PAST

ADVENTURE #5 Attend the very first rock concert! Take an awesome time machine into the Stone Age and get ready to rock!

Use information from the poster to answer the questions.

1. Who performs *My Cave's on Fire?*

 ____

2. What follows the intermission?

 ____

3. What song does Mick Jagged & the Rolling Boulders perform?

 ____

4. Which song is sung by the Smashing Marbles?

 ____

5. Who sings with Bronto?

 ____

6. What do the Limestone Lovers perform?

 ____

7. Who is the lead singer with the Hot Rocks?

 ____

8. Who performs *The Gravel Pit Rock?*

 ____

9. Who sings about a brontosaurus?

 ____

10. Where is the concert held?

 ____

11. Who performs *Dancin' at the Quarry?*

 ____

12. When does the concert begin?

 ____

13. Who sings about granite?

 ____

GRANITEVILLE MUSIC FEST

Place: Hard Rock Arena
Time: After Dark

PROGRAM

I Dino If I Love You Anymore
Mick Jagged & the Rolling Boulders

I Feel Like a Brontosaurus Stomped on my Head
The Petro Cliff Trio

Your Love Is Like a Sabre-Tooth Tiger
Terri Dactyl & the Hot Rocks

Sha-boom, Sha-boom, Sha-Rock
The Lava-Ettes

You're As Cuddly As a Woolly Mammoth
The Smashing Marbles

INTERMISSION

Be a Little Boulder, Honey
Curt McCave

The Gravel Pit Rock
The Cro-Magnon Crooners

Please Don't Take Me for Granite, Baby
The Standing Stones

My Cave's on Fire
The Paleo-Lyths

Your Heart's Made of Stone
Bronto & the Cave Dudes

Dancin' at the Quarry
Tommy Shale

I've Cried Pebbles over You
The Limestone Lovers

Till the Volcano Blows
The Square Wheels

Name ______________________________

RIDE THE BIG ONE!

ADVENTURE #6 Grab some sunscreen and your surfboard. We'll take you to Hawaii, Australia, South Africa, and South America in search of the biggest waves in the world! Travel up to 35 miles per hour on top of a wave. Insurance is included!

Read the statements about the surfers. Then answer the questions below.

Jeri wears glasses.

Jules is from Malibu.

Jess is not from Big Sur.

Jo is not from Mexico.

Jo is not from Big Sur.

Jo wears stripes when surfing.

Jamie is not from Australia.

The surfer from Maui is male.

The oldest surfer is from Malibu.

The surfer from Mexico wears glasses.

The surfer from Australia has curly hair.

Jess always wears a life vest when surfing.

________________ 1. Which surfer lives in Big Sur?

________________ 2. Which surfer is from Australia?

________________ 3. Which surfer is from Mexico?

________________ 4. Which surfer is from Maui?

________________ 5. Which surfer wears a polka-dotted suit?

Name

Theme, Summarize

FIGHT THE FIERCEST BULL

ADVENTURE #7 We'll take you straight to Madrid for a bullfighting adventure. We supply the matador costume and the red cape. You supply the bravery!

Number the lines of each limerick in the correct order. Write the theme that all the poems have in common. Then, give a spoken summary of one of the limericks to a friend.

The theme of these limericks is______________________________________

1.

____ By the creature's right horn,

____ A nervous matador named José

____ But the crowd just kept shouting, "Olé!"

____ Tried to outwit a bull yesterday.

____ His shoulder was torn

2.

____ And the people of Spain called him, "COOL"!

____ A bull had the name of Raoul

____ Anyone who would fight him was a fool.

____ His stomping was fearful,

____ And his snort was an earful.

4.

____ A man bought a bull in Madrid

____ In return for their adoring

____ So they traded him in for a squid!

____ As a pet for Alberto, his kid.

____ The bull got busy goring,

3.

____ As I did, I could hear the crowd roar.

____ And without thinking, I ran for the door!

____ And charged straight for my head,

____ Then the bull, he saw red,

____ I waved the cape, like a brave matador.

5.

____ "I can outsmart that old bull, no doubt!"

____ On a stretcher they carried her out.

____ But it sure was her worst!

____ The fight wasn't her first,

____ She said with an arrogant shout.

Name

MEET THE MAN OF LAMANCHA

ADVENTURE #8 Ride with the outlandish, mythical knight, Don Quixote, Man of la Mancha! See what fun he had on his outlandish adventures!

DRAGONS, WINDMILLS, & FIERCE ARMIES TO CONQUER

An unusual young man spent years reading wonderful tales about knighthood. His fantasies were filled with all the battles and quarrels, loves, adventures, dragons, and enchantments of the lives of knights. He read so much that his brain dried up and he got a little crazy. He decided to become a knight and do everything he had read about. He thought up an excellent, knightly name for himself: Don Quixote, Man of la Mancha.

The new knight got some old armor of his grandfather's and saddled up his weak old horse. He took Sancho, a simple neighbor, along as his squire. Off he went to have the adventures of a knight.

Soon he came upon a gang of more than thirty giants. Sancho pointed out that these were windmills, not giants, but Don Quixote rode forward bravely to fight the giants, waving his sword wildly. He broke his sword and was thrown from his horse, but he still believed he had fought giants.

Next he saw two huge armies and decided to join one and lead it to defeat the other. The armies were two flocks of sheep, but Don Quixote did not seem to notice. Waving and whirling his sword, he charged into the midst of the sheep. The shepherds thought he was crazy. They threw stones at him to drive him off. He was sure he had been wounded by the swords of the enemy in battle.

Write a short summary of the story of Don Quixote.

____

____

____

____

____

____

____

Name

THINK LIKE A DETECTIVE

ADVENTURE #9 Detectives read newspapers every day. They find all sorts of good clues in the papers. At Detective School, you'll learn to find clues too.

Skim each news report. Then write an interesting headline that summarizes the report.

1. ***Sunday Gazette***

   ____

   Fashion designer Hotzee Totzee has a new evening gown collection that is all the rage in Paris fashion circles. The gowns are made entirely of rubber, bottle caps, and feathers.

2. *Sleepyville Daily News*

   ____

   Sleepyville has recently seen a dramatic jump in the number of jaywalking violations. The city council places the blame on the increase in sidewalk sales on Main Street.

3. ***The Mail Tribune***

   ____

   The recent conflict in the tiny country of Bingo-Bingo has made relations with its two neighboring countries a bit tense. The United Nations has sent peacekeepers to the region.

4. ***The Evening News***

   ____

   Hector VonHyjack, the famous spy, has finally been caught by the CIA. After hiding for 25 years, he was found living with a false identity in the tiny town of Valport, Maine, and working as a pharmacist.

5. ***Sun City Reporter***

   ____

   World champion skier Peeper Scoot broke her own world record in downhill skiing yesterday. It was her 18th birthday.

Name ____

LEARN TO SEE RED

ADVENTURE #10. Enter into a world of red. See, touch, smell, taste, hear, feel, and think RED!

Read the writing by Ramon, Alyssa, and Jason. Finish the poem below to follow the same theme.

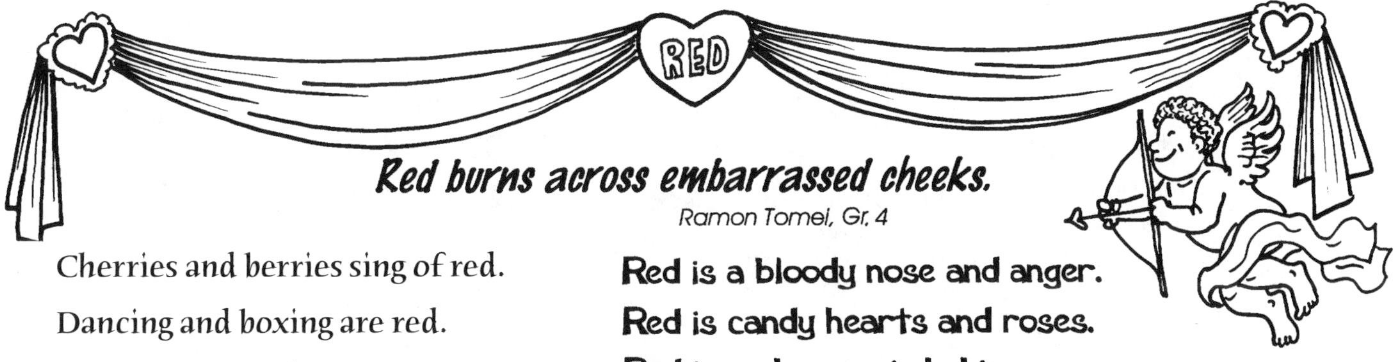

Red burns across embarrassed cheeks.

Ramon Tomei, Gr. 4

Cherries and berries sing of red.
Dancing and boxing are red.
Rock music is red.
Red is joy and laughter and summer.
Hot, hurting tears burn red in my eyes.
Rhubarb pie drips red on my shirt.
Mean words are red.

Alyssa Meyers, Gr. 5

Red is a bloody nose and anger.
Red is candy hearts and roses.
Red is a cherry pie baking,
And the smell of homemade spaghetti sauce.
I feel red when someone makes fun of me.
A cold nose feels red. So does July.
Sirens scream red, and newborn babies cry red.
Red is an argument with my brother.
Hot peppers on my tongue burn red.

Jason Williams, Gr. 5

Red is ______________, ______________, and ______________.

____________________ is red. So is ____________________.

____________________ and ____________________ sound red.

Red is the taste of ________________ and ________________.

____ feels red.

My favorite red place is __________________________________.

____ sounds red.

Red is __________________, and red is __________________.

I feel red when ____________________________________.

So is ____.

Try some *green, yellow, orange, red, black,* or *blue* writing, too!

Name ____

BRING A MASK

ADVENTURE #11 Find yourself a great costume and a wonderful mask. You're invited to be the guest of King Louis XIV at the great palace of Versailles!

On this page and the next page (page 35), read about each guest you will meet at the ball. Then answer the questions.

1. What word would you use to describe Count Pompous? ____________________
   (Do not use one that is used here.)

   What things in the description helped you choose this word?________________

   ____

   ____

2. From what you have read, tell what kind of an event this ball is.

   ____

   ____

   ____

   ____

What a jolly fellow is the friendly Jacques Joli! It's a pleasure to have his company. He has a clever, happy word for every guest.

Use with page 35.

Name

Read about these guests, too. Then answer the questions.

Lady Columbine is busy showing off her beauty and grace. She just knows that everyone is looking at her, and no one else. If you are not a young, handsome, wealthy prince, she won't want to waste her time on you!

3. What word would you use to describe Lady Columbine?

   ____

   What things in the description helped you choose this word?

   ____

   ____

   ____

4. What kinds of things would you expect Prince Mischief to do at this party?

   ____

   ____

   ____

Little Prince Mischief just loves these parties, too! He is so small that guests hardly notice him. He lurks around under tables and behind curtains, having loads of fun!

5. What guest would you most like to meet?

   ____

   Why? ______________________________

   ____

   ____

   ____

There's Dowager La-de-da! How honored you should be to come into the presence of this rich old dame. Be sure you do not say anything rowdy or improper in her presence. She has no time for foolishness.

Judge d'Éclaire is a very important man. He loves these parties because of the plentiful food. Oh, how he loves to eat! If you stop to visit with him, do bring him a pastry or two.

Use with page 34.

Name ______________________________

RIDE A FAMOUS TRAIN

ADVENTURE #12 It's the train of mystery and luxury! Ride the famous Orient Express from Paris to Istanbul. You will need to pack lightly. There's not much room for luggage in your sleeper compartment.

Examine the picture carefully. Think of an event that is about to happen on this train. Write five words to describe or name the action that each of the characters will take in the event.

The Porter ______________________________

Countess L'Orange ______________________________

Dr. Plumper ______________________________

The Mystery Man ______________________________

Madeline Merry ______________________________

Mrs. Mergatroid Matisse ______________________________

Oliver Snooze ______________________________

The Burglar ______________________________

Name ______________________________

HEAD INTO THE TANGLED WOODS

ADVENTURE #13 Take the camping trip of your life! We will drop you off in a deep, tangled forest. You can test your courage and skills. Who knows, maybe you won't really be alone out there!

Something's Coming

by Kathryn Harriss, Gr. 5

Something's coming!
Coming, coming closer!
Closer, closer still!
It walks, it talks, it stalks in the night.
Feel its breath upon your face.
Shield your eyes from its brilliant glow.
Something's coming!
Coming, coming closer!
What is it?
Who knows?

Answer the questions.

1. How is a poem different from a story?

2. Why do you think Kathryn wrote "Something's Coming"?

3. How does the poem form help with this purpose?

4. Why do you think the author wrote the lines in different lengths?

5. Why do you think Linda wrote "Far From Civilization"?

6. In each poem, circle the line or phrase that best helps the author's purpose.

Far From Civilization

by Linda NewComb, Gr. 5

I know I am far from civilization
When I hear the fish jumping
The rain hitting the tent
And
Rocks falling
When I feel the cool chill in the air
When I see the top of my west wind
Tent
And
When I smell the sweet scent of
White bark pines
And
Fresh air.
That is how I know I am
Far from civilization.

Name

WATCH THE CONFUSION

ADVENTURE #14 Visit a courtroom in confusion! Hear the different points of view. Whatever will the judge do?

Read the court cases on this page and the next page (page 39). Identify the point of view of the writer for each case.

Case #1

Five people showed up in Judge Law's courtroom today. All of us claimed to be Pat Pagoo. Pat is the person who will inherit 20 million dollars. All persons brought birth certificates to prove who they were. I know that I am Pat Pagoo. I do not know who these other people are! They are imposters! Surely the judge will see this!

1. The point of view is: ______________________

Will the real Pat Pagoo please stand up?

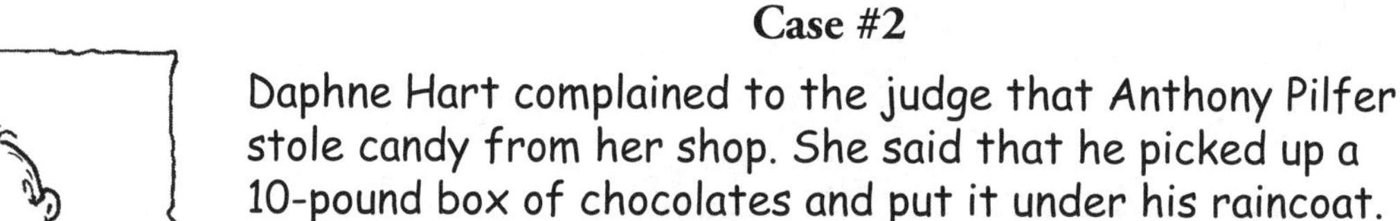

Case #2

Daphne Hart complained to the judge that Anthony Pilfer stole candy from her shop. She said that he picked up a 10-pound box of chocolates and put it under his raincoat. She claimed he slipped out the back door without paying for the candy.

Mr. Pilfer said he was allergic to chocolate. He said he was not guilty.

2. The point of view is: ______________________

Mr. Pilfer pled "not guilty."

Case #3

Mrs. Grundy is suing her neighbor, Jeb Jefferson. She wants him to pay $400 for her ruined flower bed. You should see how mad she was today in court! She says the Jefferson's dog dug up her flowers. The Jeffersons claim they do not have a dog. But you live next door to them, and you know they do!

3. The point of view is: ______________________

Mrs. Grundy swore to tell the truth.

Use with page 39.

Name

Read the rest of the court cases.
Identify the point of view of the writer for each case.

Case #4

The Cream Puff Heaven Bakery was charged with false advertising. Mr. Charles Clare buys 48 cream puffs every day. According to Mr. Clare, the bakery has been using artificial whipped cream in its puffs. He brought in the bakery's ad. This says the bakery uses real cream. The judge asked for a dozen cream puffs to sample.

4. The point of view is: ______________________________

Cream puff fakery?

Case #5

You will never believe this next case! Mr. Rush has received nine speeding tickets in one week! The judge himself has watched Mr. Rush speed down Main Street. Mr. Rush even went 20 miles per hour over the speed limit on his way to court today. Several witnesses saw this! The judge ordered him to pay fines and go to Speeder's School for a year.

5. The point of view is:

____

"Pay the fine," ordered the Judge.

A problem tree.

Case #6

I was surprised that Mrs. Abernathy did not sue the city earlier. Today she did. The city ordered her to cut down a dying tree that sits in front of her house. She claims the tree belongs to the city because its roots are under the city street. I live near Mrs. Abernathy. That tree is a hazard! I was glad that the judge agreed with her.

6. The point of view is: ______________________________

Use with page 38.

Name

MEET THE GREATEST COWBOY

ADVENTURE #15 Join the wild escapades of the great cowboy hero, Pecos Bill! Ride a cyclone, tame rattlesnakes, and learn to lasso a speeding train!

Read the tale. Answer the question. Then follow the instructions on the next page (page 41) to compare the written tale to the pictures that tell the tale.

A TALL COWBOY TALE

Pecos Bill was the greatest cowboy of all—a hero to all cowboys. When he was a baby, he fell out of his family's wagon and was left behind along the Pecos River. A family of coyotes adopted him, and he thought he was a coyote for many years.

Some cowboys found him and took him in. They taught him cowboy skills. He grew to be so big and strong and brave, that he could do far more than the other cowboys.

Bill was eight feet tall and carried seven guns and nine knives in his belt. He could ride the biggest, most powerful horses. No horse could throw him. He could ride anything—no matter how wild. One time he rode a mountain lion, using a rattlesnake as a whip. Another time, he rode a wild cyclone!

One day, two rattlesnakes bothered Bill. He grabbed one in each hand and shook the daylights out of them. Then he tied their tails together and hung them in a tree.

Pecos Bill could lasso whole herds of cattle at one time. He could lasso anything! The best trick he ever did happened the day he spied a runaway train. Bill just grabbed his lasso, and lassoed that train!

Yes, Pecos Bill is still talked about in cowboy country. If you go to the Arizona desert, you will still see the footprints that his huge horses left among the rocks.

1. What makes this a tall tale?
   (Give some examples from the text.)

Use with page 41.

Name

Look at the pictures that tell the tale of Pecos Bill. (See pictures on this page and page 40). Compare the written tale to the picture tale.

2. What did you learn or experience from the pictures that you did not get from the written tale?

____

____

____

____

____

____

____

3. What did you learn or experience from the written tale that you did not get from the pictures?

____

____

____

____

____

____

____

Use with page 40.

Name

HOLD ON TO YOUR STOMACH!

ADVENTURE #16 Be one of the first to ride *The Stomach-Grabber*—a new, huge, terrifying roller coaster. Don't choose this adventure unless you have a stomach of iron!

THIRTEEN THRILLS on THIRTEEN HILLS

You have waited in line for two hours to ride the new upside-down, triple loop, heart-stopping rollercoaster. It has thirteen awesome hills. While you wait, you begin to imagine the screams and screeches you'll soon be hearing.

You are nervous, excited, impatient to get on. You trust this rollercoaster, or you wouldn't be trying it out. Even though you're the first customer to ride, you are sure it will be safe. When it's time to ride, you don't care how it works. You just want to get on!

A moving chain will pull the car to the top. When the car gets to the peak of the hill and starts to curve over, gravity pulls it down the steep incline. At the very top of each hill, your body keeps going up out of your seat because of inertia. You feel like you are flying, but soon the gravity has you back in your seat again. At every curve and every upside-down loop, centripetal force pushes you against your seat. This is why you don't fall out. Finally, friction slows down the coaster and stops it.

The ride is over. You enjoyed every minute of it. Your stomach feels great, and you want to ride again right away!

Go on to read the poem about *The Stomach-Grabber* on the next page (page 43). Then answer the questions to compare the two texts.

1. What do you notice about the structure of the text on this page ("Thirteen Thrills on Thirteen Hills)? ____

   ____

2. What is the structure of the text on the next page: "A Ride for the Brave and Bold"? ___

   ____

   ____

3. What is the author's purpose for "Thirteen Thrills on Thirteen Hills"?______________

   ____

Use with page 43.

Name ____

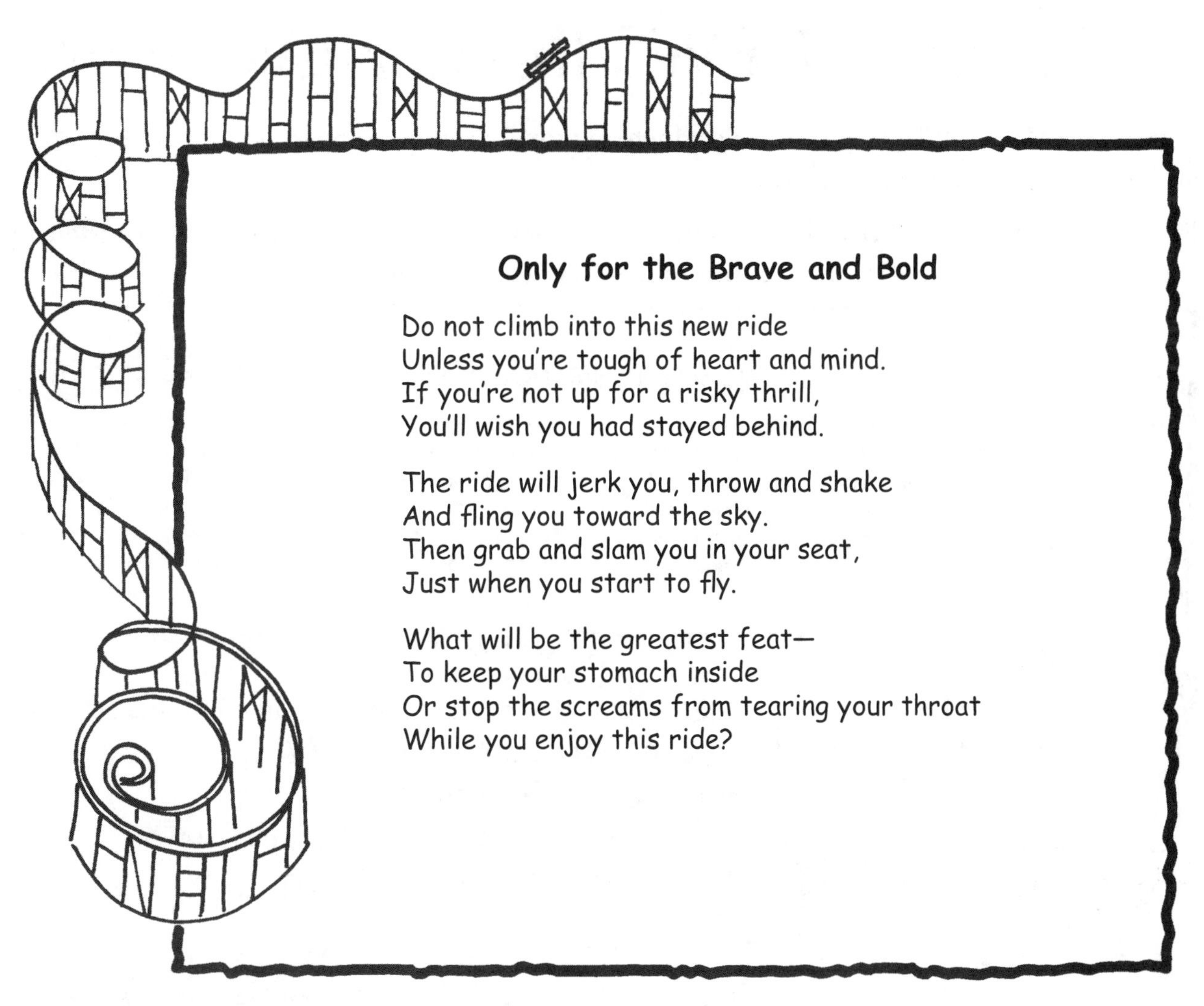

Only for the Brave and Bold

Do not climb into this new ride
Unless you're tough of heart and mind.
If you're not up for a risky thrill,
You'll wish you had stayed behind.

The ride will jerk you, throw and shake
And fling you toward the sky.
Then grab and slam you in your seat,
Just when you start to fly.

What will be the greatest feat—
To keep your stomach inside
Or stop the screams from tearing your throat
While you enjoy this ride?

Read the text on page 42 along with this poem.
Then answer the questions to compare the two texts.

4. How does the author's purpose for "Only for the Brave and Bold" compare to the author's purpose for "Thirteen Thrills on Thirteen Hills"?______________________________

____

____

5. What impression did you get from the prose text (page 42) that is different from the impression you got from the poem (page 43)? ______________________________

____

____

____

____

Use with page 42.

Name

TURN OLD NEWS INTO NEW NEWS

ADVENTURE #17 Drop into a world where nursery rhymes turn to news. Turn any old familiar story into today's headlines.

Read the story of Jack Sprat in different forms. Next to each one, write a note to identify the form. Be ready to discuss the differences between the forms.

COUPLE SUFFERS STRANGE DISEASE

City Center Hospital admitted a man and his wife today. Each suffers from a rare eating disorder. The man, Mr. Jack Sprat, of 1616 Hambone Lane, has a condition that makes it impossible for him to eat anything but meat. His wife, Maryanne Sprat, of the same address, says she can eat nothing but fat. Both of them are being tested by medical experts who are looking for the cause of their ailments. Doctors are puzzled about how to treat the couple. Mr. Sprat had a positive outlook. "One good thing," he said, "no food is wasted in our household!"

WANT AD

WANTED:
Man that can eat no fat seeks girlfriend who eats no meat. Call 555-0001 after 3 P.M.

LIMERICK

There once was a young man named Sprat
Whose wife could eat only fat
But one day he found
That she craved some ground round
And it started a horrible spat!

Dear Maryanne,
I cannot take it any more! Night after night I sit with my boring, lean chicken or steak and watch while you delight with your French fries and cream puffs, fudgy ice cream and rich gravy. I have to confess that I crave those rich, fatty foods you eat. I must try them. I beg you, please trade places with me for just one night!
Your loving, starving husband,
Jack

ODE

Ode to a Burger
Oh, how I'd love to taste you
Once...If only I could
You know that I would!
I'd love to savor
Your charcoal flavor
To slurp those juices you've got...
But, alas, I cannot!

Two twins with tricky tastes never tasted two tastes.

Name

READING

INFORMATIONAL TEXT

Grade 4

TAKE LESSONS IN SILLINESS

ADVENTURE #18 Spend a month at Clown College—and learn a lot about clowning around.

Read the titles of the books that clowns in training must read. Write the letter of the book in which you would expect to learn each of these skills below. Be ready to explain your choices.

_____ 1. how to make clown faces

_____ 2. complicated jokes

_____ 3. how to keep from injuring your back during somersaults

_____ 4. jokes, when you know none

_____ 5. how to choose your first costume

_____ 6. what to do about a bad rash on your nose

_____ 7. how to make your nose look great

_____ 8. how to fix a flat tire on your unicycle

_____ 9. tricks to do with balloons

_____ 10. funny ways to move your body

_____ 11. how to walk with big feet

_____ 12. why clowns have big feet

_____ 13. how to get nine clowns on a skateboard

_____ 14. getting makeup out of your eyes

A. CLOWN NOSES EVERYTHING YOU NEED TO KNOW

B. The Complete Collection of BEST JOKES Beginner to Advanced

C. Creative Costumes

D. the 300 WORST CLOWNING INJURIES Prevention Guide

E. a short history of BIG Feet!

F. Unicycle maintenance A 12-STEP MANUAL

G. A CLOWN'S HAND BOOK OF TRICKS

H. MAKEUP GUIDE FOR UNIQUE CLOWN FACES

Name

RACE WITH THE DOGS

ADVENTURE #19 Bring your warmest clothes to Alaska, because you'll be driving a team of racing sled dogs over a snow-covered course! You might even get good enough to join the toughest race of all: the Iditarod International Sled Dog Race.

Read the weather reports for the first six days of the Iditarod. Then answer the questions below. Circle the part of the text that helps you answer each question.

DAY 1: WEATHER REPORT
The skies will be clear today, with temperatures at 0°. Light, fluffy snow covers the ground.

DAY 2: WEATHER REPORT
Temperatures are warming. Expect a light rain, which will turn to freezing rain this afternoon.

DAY 3: WEATHER REPORT
Heavy fog will move in, bringing moist, wet air hovering over the snow. Winds will be harsh this evening.

DAY 4: WEATHER REPORT
Extreme blizzard conditions are reported today. Warnings are out for complete white-out conditions. Winds are blowing at 60 mph with drifts up to six feet.

DAY 5: WEATHER REPORT
Today the temperatures will climb to 20° with light snow showers and light winds.

DAY 6: WEATHER REPORT
Temperatures have taken a plunge. At noon, we recorded –25° with a –80° wind chill factor. Everyone is warned to stay indoors. It is extremely dangerous for people or animals to be outdoors in these conditions.

1. On what day might the racers have the best conditions? ____________________
2. If ice is a problem, what day(s) might give the racers problems? ____________________
3. What troubles might the drivers and dogs have on Day 4? ____________________

   ____
4. What troubles might they have on Day 3? ____________________

   ____
5. What kind of progress do you think they'll make on Day 5? ____________________
6. What do you think the racing teams will do on Day 6? ____________________

Name ____

TRY AN ANCIENT ART

1 Remove the brain and throw it away.

2 Remove the internal organs and save them in canopic jars.

LUNGS STOMACH LIVER INTESTINES

3 Pack the body cavity with an embalming chemical called natron.

4 Cover the body with a mud pack of natron to dry it out. Let the body dry for 40 days.

5 Wrap the body in strips of linen moistened with resin glue.

6 The wrapping is finished after 20 or more layers.

7 The mummy is placed into 3 coffins.

#1 #2 #3

ADVENTURE #20

Learn to make a mummy! Travel back to ancient Egypt and get a lesson in one of the most unusual ideas of all time. This adventure is not for the weak-hearted. If you try it, you'll never forget the experience!

Answer each question and write the step number that helped with your answer.

A. How long is the body covered with natron ? ______________

B. What does the natron do to the body? ______________ ______________

C. How many layers of linen and resin are wrapped around the body? ______________

D. What is saved in jars? ______________

E. What is thrown away ? ______________

F. What is the last step in making the mummy? ______________

G. Which part of the process looks the hardest? ______________
Tell why. ______________

Name ______________

CLIMB "THE GREAT ONE"

ADVENTURE #21 Climb the Great Denali in the center of the Alaska Mountain Range. Denali is the native American name for Mt. McKinley—the highest mountain in North America. You'll need lots of training and equipment because this is 20,320 feet high!

Read the posters from climbing supply shops. Answer the questions.

USED EQUIPMENT
picks
sleeping bags
tents
maps
camping stoves

GREAT DEALS!
Mountain Supply
552-9900

THE
ULTIMATE
TENT
See it! Try it!
100% waterproof
lightweight shelter
easy to set up in snow!
double sewn seams
weight—4 lbs
ON SALE, NOW

Climber's Shop
1000 Broad St.

DVD
CLIMBING DENALI
See the climb before you do it!
$20.00
Video Stop Shop
550-2980

ZOOM
HEADLAMP
Best one on the market!
$39
Saturday Only
Camping Ltd.
201 First St.

CARABINERS
you can count on
New 3-D shape
Every one
tested!
Lightweight!

Stop & see them!
Mountain Store
3910 Abby Lane

SLEEPING
BAGS
for cold places
100% fine goose down
Good to –60°
High Quality design
ALL BAGS
30% OFF

Camping, Ltd.
201 First St.

1. What is the weight of the ultimate tent? ______________________________
2. Are used climbing ropes advertised? ____
3. What product is advertised as having a 3-D shape? ______________________
4. Which products are advertised as lightweight? ____________________
5. Where can you buy a product that is 100% waterproof? ____________________
6. What would you pay for a ZOOM headlamp and the DVD? ____________
7. Where is the Mountain Store located? ______________________________
8. What can you see on the advertised DVD? ______________________________
9. Where can you buy maps? ______________________________
10. What store is on First Street? ______________________________
11. How many stores have phone numbers advertised? ____________________
12. What phone number would you call to ask about camping stoves? ____________
13. Where can you buy carabiners? ________
14. How much money would you save on a $250 sleeping bag at Camping, Ltd? ______
15. What is the lowest temperature for the sleeping bags at Camping, Ltd? ________

Name ______________________________

Explain Ideas from Text

STAY IN MOTION

ADVENTURE #22 A scientist named Newton wrote down some things that were learned long ago about motion. These are called Newton's Laws of Motion. This adventure puts you in the middle of the motion. You can actually experience Newton's laws!

Read the Laws of Motion. Read each kid's description of what he or she is doing. Explain what made him or her do that! Also, write the number of the law.

LAW #1 Any moving object will keep moving in the same direction at the same speed unless some force changes its direction or speed.

LAW #2 Any object speeds up or slows down in proportion to the size of the force acting on it.

LAW #3 For any action, there is an equal and opposite reaction.

1. What made me do that? Law # ______________________

   Explain: ______________________

2. What made me do that? Law # ______________________

   Explain: ______________________

3. What made me do that? Law # ______________________

   Explain: ______________________

Use with page 51.

Name ______________________

Explain Ideas from Text

Read the Laws of Motion. Read each kid's description of what he or she is doing. Explain what made him or her do that! Also, write the number of the law.

4. What made me do that? Law # ______________________________

   Explain: ______________________________

5. What made me do that? Law # ______________________________

   Explain: ______________________________

6. What made me do that? Law # ______________________________

   Explain: ______________________________

Use with page 50.

Name ______________________________

Main Idea, Summarize

TRY TRICKS ON THE SLOPES

ADVENTURE #23 Learn downhill tricks from the champions! All kinds of fantastic antics happen on the slopes in the Winter Olympic Games. Here's your chance to learn some tricks from the best athletes!

Read the text about each Olympic event. Below the text, write the main idea of the text.

1. In the halfpipe event, snowboarders zip up and down the steep sides of a halfpipe. It is a U-shaped trench carved out of snow. Halfpipe competitors do wild tricks with crazy names like Ollies, Chicken Salad, McTwist, and Fakies.

The main idea of the passage is

____

____

2. USA's Picabo Street won a silver medal in downhill racing at the 1994 Olympics. Then she injured her knee badly in 1996, but came back to win a gold medal in the Super-Giant Slalom at the 1998 games in Japan.

The main idea of the passage is

____

____

3. Aerial skiing contests are great fun! Daring skiers perform flips and twists in the air off a 66-yard long ramp. Judges give them a score that is based 20% on the takeoff, 50% on the flight in the air, and 30% on the landing.

The main idea of the passage is

____

____

4. Ski jumpers fly through the air with their ski-tips spread apart in a V-style. This V gives them greater lift from the air as the air flows beneath the skis. This helps the skiers fly farther. Nasahiko Harada, from Japan, is one of the best ski jumpers ever.

The main idea of the passage is

____

____

5. Which of these best summarizes the idea of all the text together? (Circle one.)

   a. Skiers do a lot of tricks in the Winter Olympics.

   b. Olympic winter snow sports include a lot of speed and tricks. Sometimes athletes get injured.

   c. Olympic athletes train very hard for many years.

   d. Sports in the Winter Olympics have crazy tricks with funny names.

Name _______________________________

VISIT MYSTERIOUS ATLANTIS

ADVENTURE #24 Climb aboard a submarine to search the oceans for the lost city of Atlantis. People wonder if Atlantis really existed. You can help to solve the mystery once and for all!

1.

Atlantis was a large mythical island in the Atlantic Ocean. Plato, a writer in ancient Greece, wrote a tale about this island. The tale told of a great empire that existed on Atlantis. In the tale, earthquakes, floods, and great storms shook the whole island. During the great storms, the island sank into the sea.

Circle the main idea of the paragraph.

a) Plato was a great writer.
b) Atlantis is a mythical island that disappeared into the sea.
c) Many tales have been told about Atlantis.
d) Earthquakes have destroyed many islands in the ocean.

2.

For centuries, people were fascinated with Plato's tales about the island of Atlantis. Many wondered where it was and how it sank. Many wondered if it was a real place or just another Greek myth. Perhaps it really existed at one time. Over the years, many stories and fantasies have been told about a great city that lies beneath the ocean. Some think that it is still inhabited by sea creatures such as mermaids and mermen. Some scientists think the tales were inspired by a real island, the island of Thira in the Aegean Sea. This island was destroyed by a volcanic eruption in 1500 B.C.

Circle the main idea of the paragraph.

a) There are many questions and theories about the existence and fate of Atlantis.
b) Many people think sea creatures still live in Atlantis.
c) The island of Atlantis was destroyed by a volcano.

3.

The great mythical empire of Atlantis was built on an island in the Atlantic Ocean. Atlantis had powerful armies which planned to conquer all of the lands in the Mediterranean area. They had success in parts of Europe and North Africa, but the armies of Athens defeated them and drove them away.

Circle the main idea of the paragraph.

a) Atlantis had powerful armies.
b) Athens had powerful armies.
c) Armies of Atlantis tried to conquer other lands.

Name

EXPLORE THE SUNKEN *TITANIC*

ADVENTURE #25 Join the underwater explorers as they unlock the mysteries of this great ship, the *Titanic.*

In the space following each paragraph, write a short summary of the main idea in that paragraph.

THE VOYAGE OF THE TITANIC

They called it "unsinkable," but the *Titanic* was not. They called it a floating luxury hotel, and indeed it was! It was like a huge palace, with huge rooms, gold-plated light fixtures, a swimming pool, and steam baths. No ship this big or beautiful had ever been built before! Hundreds of passengers and families boarded the *Titanic* in Southampton, England, on April 10, 1912. The great new ship was bound for New York on its maiden voyage.

____

____

At a half hour past midnight on April 15, 1912, disaster struck the *Titanic*. Actually, the ship struck disaster—in the form of an iceberg. At first, passengers didn't realize that the accident was serious. There was a command for people to get into the lifeboats. Unfortunately, the company that built the boat was so convinced it was unsinkable that they had sent lifeboats for only about half the people on board.

____

____

The ship sent out distress signals, hoping nearby ships would come to help. The bow of the Titanic was sinking when a loud, roaring noise went up from the ship. The *Titanic* was breaking apart. It stood up in the air for a short while, and then disappeared beneath the waves. The next day, another ship, the *Carpathia*, came to rescue many survivors. Survivors included 712 passengers and crew members. Hundreds did not survive.

____

____

There are many theories about why the *Titanic* sank. Seventy-five years after the sinking, and after much searching, the wreckage of the *Titanic* was found. Small submarines have explored the wreckage. Maybe some of the mysteries will now be solved.

____

____

____

Name

VISIT WITH A PLANT

ADVENTURE #26 Get to know plants up close! Sit for 24 hours with a plant and watch its cycle of vital processes. Plants give us good air! They even recycle air for us.

What processes are shown by each picture? Write one of these labels above each picture: Transpiration, Respiration, or Photosynthesis. Then fill in the blanks below with the science words to describe each process.

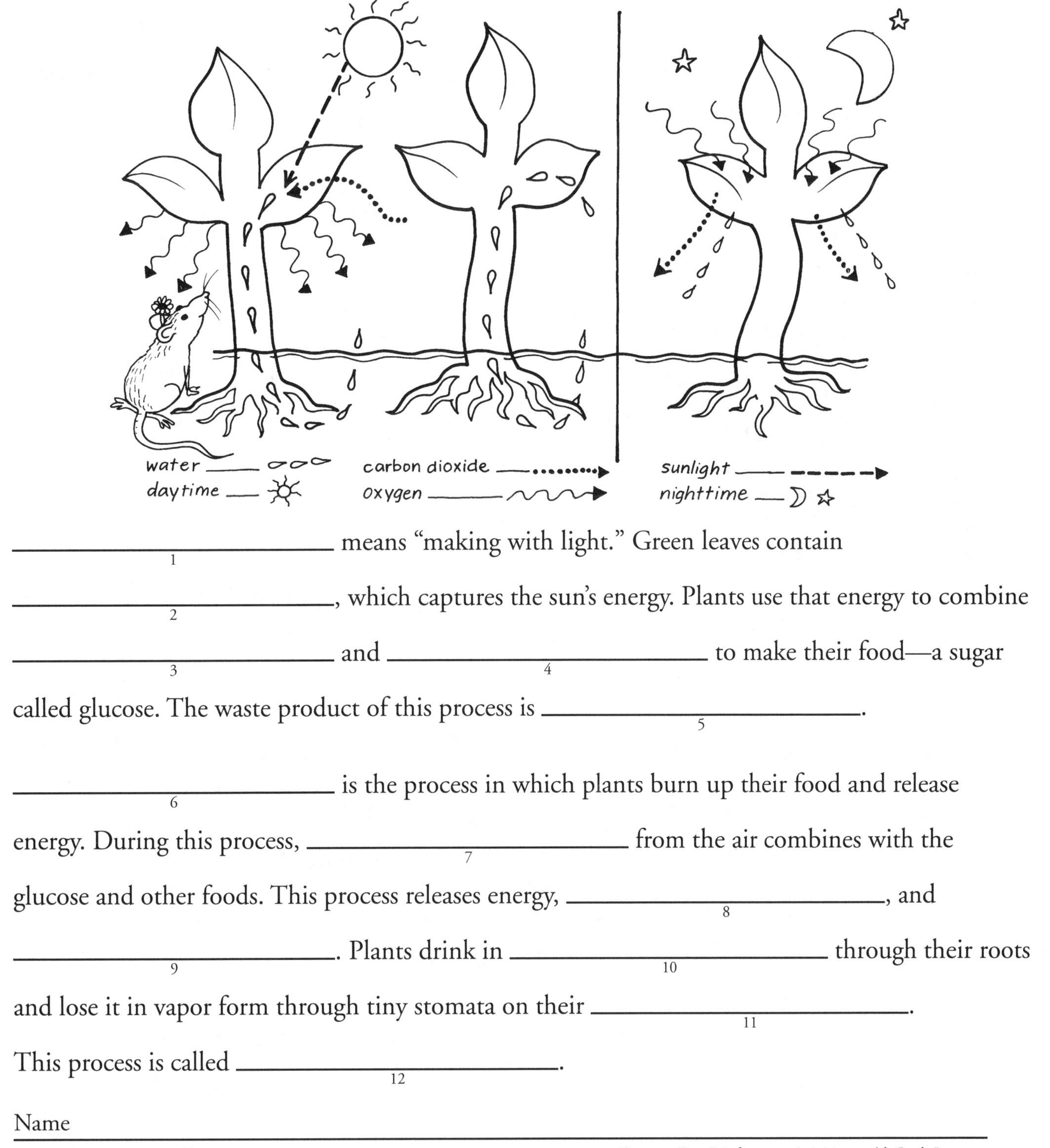

__________ (1) means "making with light." Green leaves contain __________ (2), which captures the sun's energy. Plants use that energy to combine __________ (3) and __________ (4) to make their food—a sugar called glucose. The waste product of this process is __________ (5).

__________ (6) is the process in which plants burn up their food and release energy. During this process, __________ (7) from the air combines with the glucose and other foods. This process releases energy, __________ (8), and __________ (9). Plants drink in __________ (10) through their roots and lose it in vapor form through tiny stomata on their __________ (11).

This process is called __________ (12).

Name __________

CONTROL THE DAMAGE

ADVENTURE #27 Rescue the work damaged by a naughty rat. Liverwort has munched on Dr. dePlant's notebook. Too bad she left her important notes in the same lab with the rats! You'll need to know some basic facts and vocabulary about ecology.

Fill in all the missing words that Liverwort has eaten.
Use words from the box below.

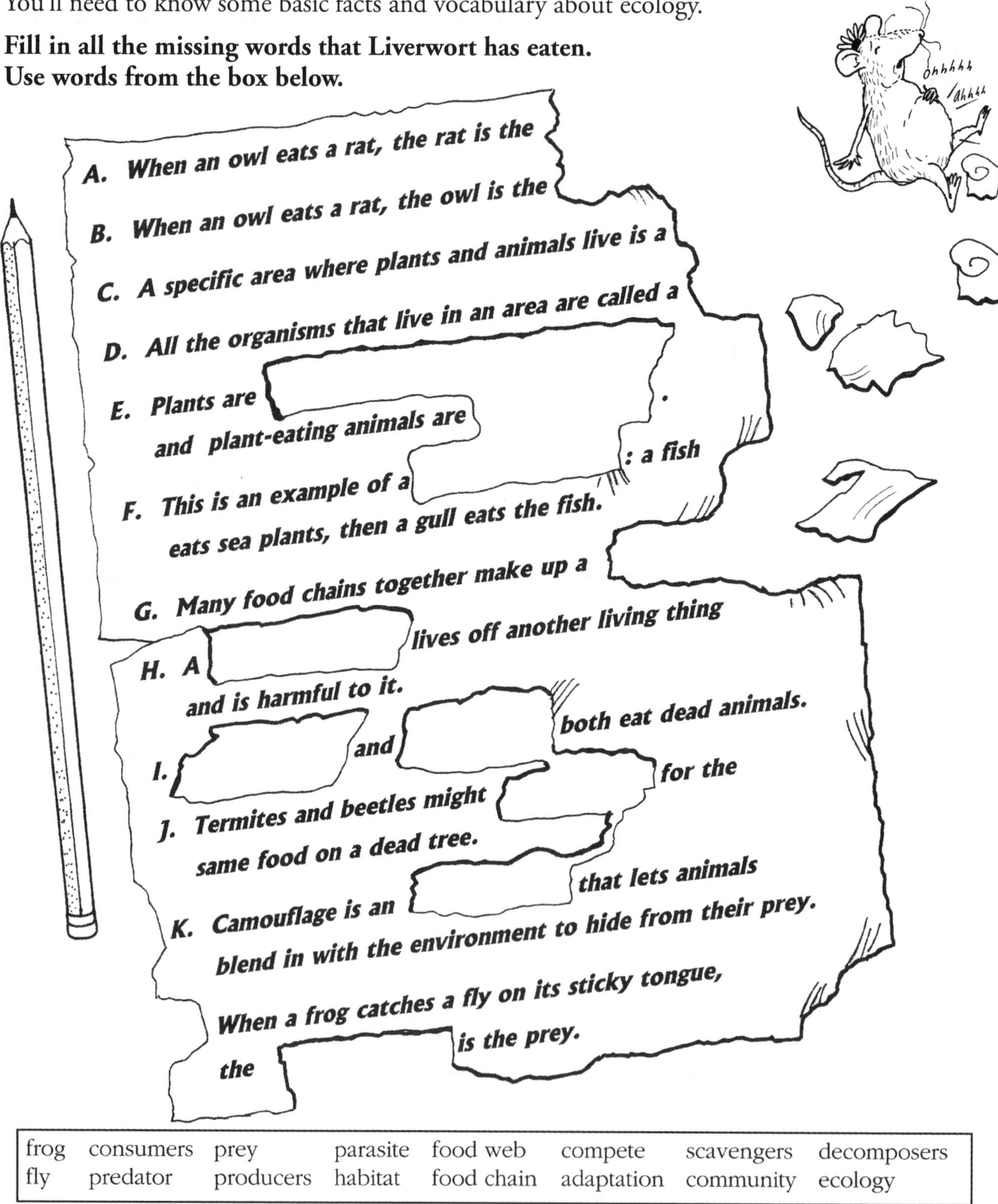

frog	consumers	prey	parasite	food web	compete	scavengers	decomposers
fly	predator	producers	habitat	food chain	adaptation	community	ecology

Name

JOIN A SPACE MISSION

ADVENTURE #28 Fly a shuttle through space to visit the Mir Space Station. This is the place where astronaut Shannon Lucid set an American space duration record in 1996. You don't have to stay as long as she did! (She stayed for more than 188 days!)

Notice how the brochure is structured. Get ready to share orally your ideas about how the information is given in a way that helps readers learn about the space station. Make notes on the page to show features of the text.

You'll be so glad you did this!!

Travel to Mir by Space Shuttle

- *Orbit the Earth & see fantastic sights!*
- *Astronauts will enjoy your visit!*
- *See the 6-port docking system.*
- *Explore the living and working spaces.*
- *Get fitted with your own space suit.*
- *Walk in space.*
- *All food and equipment are provided.*
- *You'll love the food!*
- *You'll have fun feeling weightless!*
- *No dangers or accidents will occur.*

All astronauts & cosmonauts want a chance to live on Mir!

Must be at least 25 years of age.

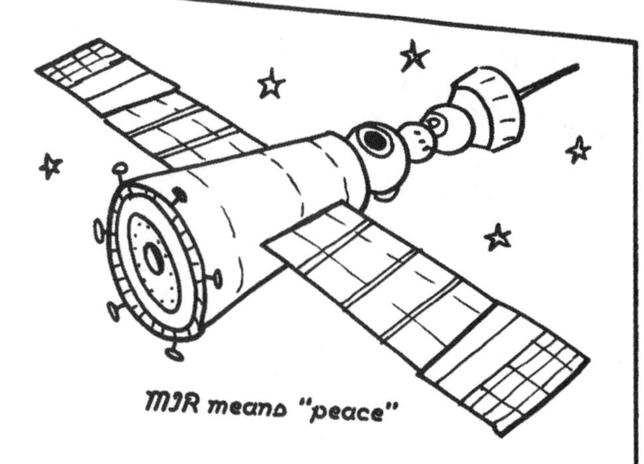

MIR means "peace"

WE PROVIDE TRAINING!

STAY 5, 10, or 15 days

We won't keep you as long as we kept Cosmonaut Aleksandr Laveikin. He stayed 326 days!

Mir was launched in 1986 by the Soviet Union. Today it is maintained by Russia.

Schedule	
TRAINING	January 1
LAUNCH	December 5
RETURN FLIGHTS	December 9
	December 14
	December 19

Adventures, Unlimited

You can afford it!
See your Adventure Company Representative

Health examination required.

Name

SOLVE UNSOLVED MYSTERIES

ADVENTURE #29 Be a detective for a day. Try to crack some unsolved mystery cases!

Read about three mysteries on this page. A narrator tells the story and the clues. On the next page, a witness to each event tells the story.

Pay careful attention to both versions. Compare the two. Get ready to solve at least one of the mysteries!

Use with page 59.

Name

Read the witness reports of the mysterious events from page 58.

For each event, make a list of differences you see between the witness report and the report on page 58. Use extra paper if you need to.

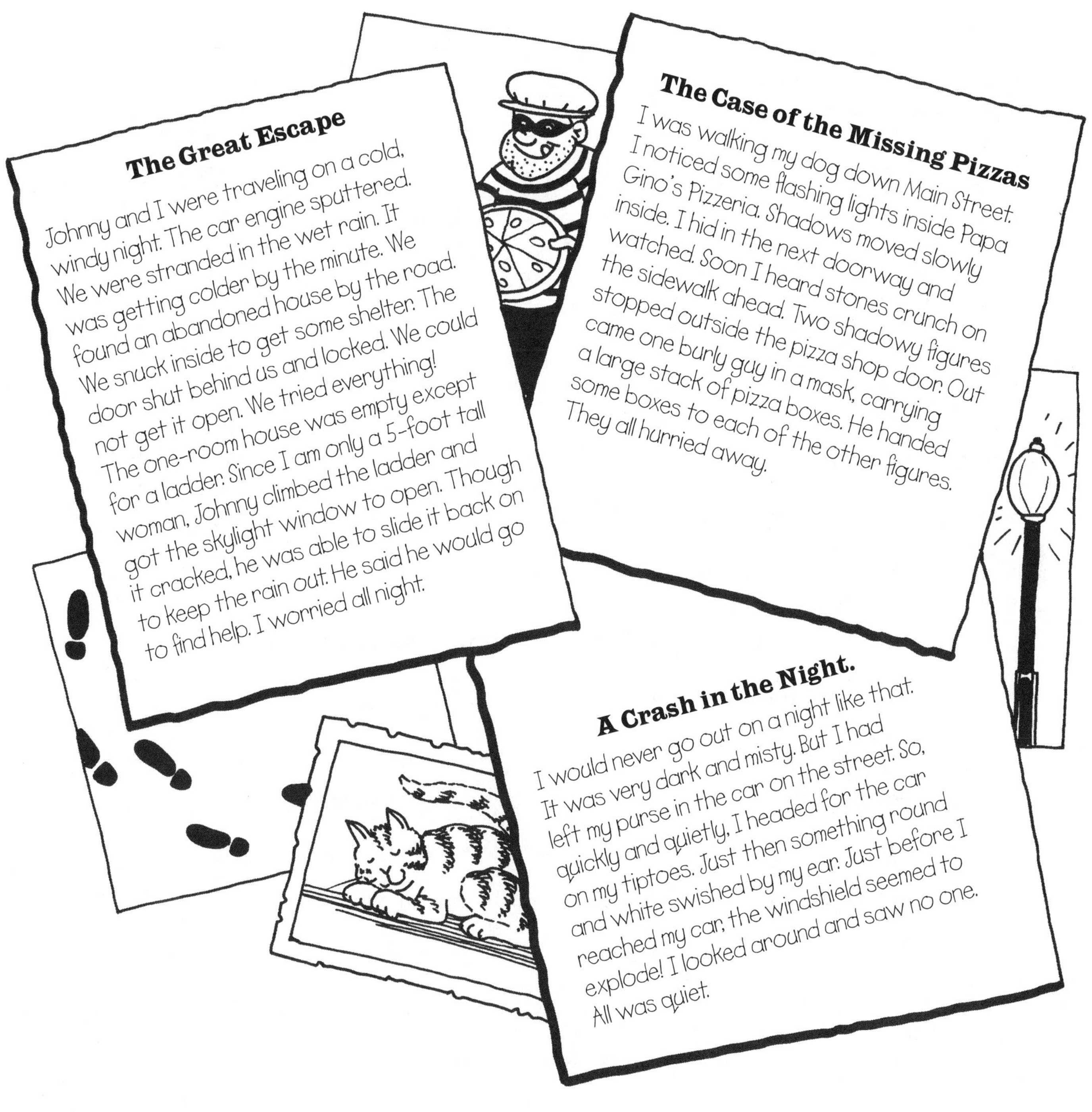

Use with page 58.

Name

TAKE A RIDE WITH THE "KING"

Most Expensive Items
of Rock Stars' Belongings Sold at Auctions

Item	Year of Sale	Price
John Lennon's 1965 Rolls-Royce Phantom V touring limousine	1985	$ 2,299,000
Jimi Hendrix's Fender Stratocaster electric guitar	1990	$ 370,260
An acoustic guitar that had been owned by George Michael, Paul McCartney, and David Bowie	1994	$ 341,000
Buddy Holly's Gibson electric guitar	1990	$ 242,000
John Lennon's 1970 Mercedes-Benz 600 limousine	1989	$ 213,125
Elvis Presley's 1942 Martin D-18 guitar	1991	$ 180,000
Elvis Presley's 1960 Rolls-Royce Phantom V touring limousine	1986	$ 162,800
Charlie Parker's Grafton saxophone	1991	$ 144,925
John Lennon's recording of his singing at a 1957 church fair	1994	$ 121,675
Buddy Holly's Fender Stratocaster electric guitar	1990	$ 110,000

ADVENTURE #30 This one will take a bit of time travel. We'll take you back to the 1960s for a ride in the Rolls Royce. A lot of Elvis fans will be jealous of you!

Use the information from the chart to answer the questions below.

1. What was the highest-price item bought before 1994? ____________________
2. Which sold for more: Elvis' car or his guitar? ____________________
3. What item sold that was neither a car nor a musical instrument? ____________________
4. In general, what kinds of items are featured in this text? ____________________
5. How does the table form of the text help a reader read the information? ____________________

____

____

____

____

Name ____________________

FOLLOW A CRIME-LINE

ADVENTURE #31 Spend some time with the great crime professor, Dr. Iam Shrewd. Learn how to make a crime-line timeline to help solve the stickiest crimes.

Professor Shrewd investigated the disappearance of a rare book from Ms. Rathskeller's shop, *Blue Dragon Used Books.* He created this timeline to record information he found. Use the timeline to answer the questions.

TIMELINE

7:59 a.m.	Ms. Rathskeller puts an ***Open*** sign in the window of her store.
8:01 a.m.	She unlocks the door.
8:04 a.m.	She goes to fix her morning cup of jasmine tea in the back room.
8:10 a.m.	Mr. Fiddle, the first customer of the day, comes in to pick up a parcel.
8:15 a.m.	Ms. Rathskeller unlocks the rare book display case to dust articles.
8:20 a.m.	Mr. Fiddle leaves to catch his bus.
8:21 a.m.	Ms. Rathskeller gets her first phone call of the day from the bank.
8:25 a.m.	The second customer of the day (an unknown person) comes in to ask directions to the post office, and leaves.
8:30 a.m.	Ms. Rathskeller goes into the back room to rinse out her teacup. She hears the bell jingle on the door.
8:32 a.m.	She comes out to see the third customer of the day, who purchases an inexpensive paperback.
8:35 a.m.	She receives her second phone call, requesting information on a book. She has to go and look it up in the card catalog.
8:38 a.m.	The third customer leaves.
8:42 a.m.	She discovers the rare book is missing from the unlocked case and calls the police.

1. What time was the first phone call of the day? ____________________
2. How long did the first customer stay in the store? ____________________
3. How long was the second customer in the store? ____________________
4. How long did the third customer stay in the store? ____________________
5. What time did Mr. Fiddle arrive at the shop? ____________________
6. The rare bookcase was opened at what time? ____________________
7. What time does she discover the rare book missing? ____________________
8. Does the third customer leave before or after the second phone call? ____________________
9. When did Ms. Rathskeller unlock the door? ____________________
10. How long was Mr. Fiddle in the shop before the case was opened? ____________________
11. Who do you think stole the rare book, and why do you think so? ____________________

____

Name ____

Interpret Visual Information

RETRIEVE A LONG-LOST RUBY

ADVENTURE #31 An anonymous call has given the location of a long-lost jewel. This ruby has been missing for over a century. It's the valuable Ruby of Amyr Khayat! Join famous Detective Gumshoe to see if the caller is right about the ruby's location!

Read each direction carefully. Use a red marker to trace the route Gary will follow.

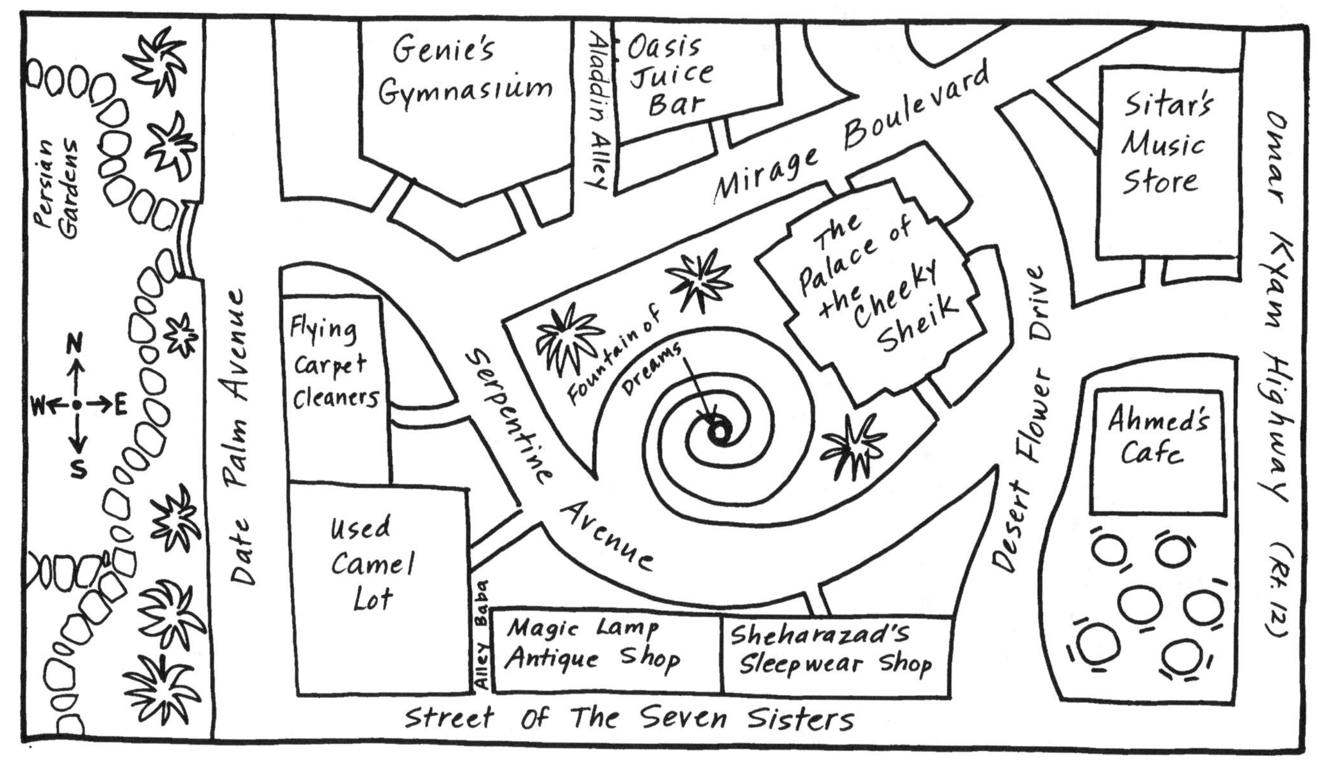

1. At exactly 11:03 P.M. on Tuesday, leave the entrance to the Persian Gardens and go south on Date Palm Avenue to the Used Camel Lot.
2. Pretend to be interested in a used camel. Then slip across Alley Baba to the Magic Lamp Antique Shop.
3. Ask for the salesman named Omar. He will direct you to Sheharazad's Sleepware Shop.
4. Look for a secret message in the silk pajamas. The message will tell you to leave the shop and go west on Serpentine Avenue, then around the Mystery Spiral to the Fountain of Dreams.
5. Wait until you hear the gong at 11:30 P.M. Head NW from the fountain, walking between the two palm trees.
6. Cross Mirage Boulevard. Go down Aladdin Alley and enter the back door of the Oasis Juice Bar.
7. Ask for a salami sandwich. The owner will send you back to Mirage Boulevard, and tell you to turn right on Desert Flower Drive and go south to Ahmed's Café.
8. Sit down at the center table. Don't look suspicious. Order a salami sandwich and a box of Turkish taffy. Ask the waitress to offer a piece of candy to the lady in red at the table directly SE of yours.
9. If the lady eats the candy, she is the one who will give you the fabulous Ruby of Amyr Khayat.

Name

CATCH A THIEF

ADVENTURE #33 Have you ever investigated an art heist? Here's your chance! The vile art thief Viva has struck again. The police have put her into a lineup of suspects. They have collected statements from witnesses who saw her leave the museum.

Read the descriptions. Don't forget that sometimes the statements of witnesses disagree with one another. Decide which suspect is Viva. Color her outfit. Discuss how you made your decision.

Name

GET A LITTLE SLUGGISH

ADVENTURE #34 It may be the only slug race in the world. Would you want to miss it? Travel into the giant redwoods of California for one of the most unusual races you'll ever see. You get front row seats. You can even race a slug if you want to!

Morning Edition

Daily News

Valley Weather: Partly Cloudy

Vol. XXXIX No 14235 Sunny Valley, California July 10, 2012 35¢

SLUG RACES COMING TO AREA SOON

There's more wildlife to watch and enjoy next month in the Pacific Coast redwoods of Northern California.

Visitors flock to Prairie Creek Redwoods State Park on the Pacific Ocean for many reasons. After they play in the ocean, they can watch elk, bears, bobcats, and foxes, which are plentiful in the ancient forest park. Campers can park trailers and hike the beautiful trails through the canyons to the ocean.

But next month, there will be another fascinating reason to visit the park. In August, the park will be the setting of the Annual Slug Derby. A variety of races will be held and prizes will be awarded to winning slugs in several categories.

One of last year's top winning banana slugs poses with her owner and her trophy. Over seven hundred spectators watched the races last year.

Two hundred trophies made by locals will be given. There will be food and fun for everyone.

Visitors are invited to attend the derby. "You can bring your own slug, or we'll loan you one from our slugarium at the visitors' center," says Park Ranger Robert Roberts. Park rangers have already started hunting for speedy slugs. Visitors need to know, however, that this is a very competitive race. Therefore, any slugs brought in from the outside will be given a slug drug test before they are eligible to take part in the races.

For information about the Banana Slug Derby, call the Prairie Creek Park Visitor's Center at 707-488-2171.

Answer the questions on this page and the next page (page 65).

1. How does the author let you know that there is wildlife to enjoy in the redwoods of Northern California?

___

___

2. Is the public welcome to watch the slug races? ________________ How do you know?

___

___

Use with page 65.

Name

Read the news article on page 64. Then answer the questions on page 64 and on this page.

3. The article says that the Banana Slug Derby is a "fascinating" reason to visit the state park. How does the article support this idea?

4. The article says that "this is a very competitive race." How does the writer support this idea?

5. From the article, would you expect this event to be a short one or a long one? ________________
How did the text help you with your answer?

Use with page 64.

Name

VISIT CAMELOT

ADVENTURE #35 Meet King Arthur. Visit Camelot. Get your very own suit of mail. Learn to fight a dragon, if you wish. Many have dreamed of this adventure. You can actually live it!

Sir Prance-a-lot is caught in the depths of a terrible dungeon, fighting a fire-breathing dragon. The dragon has wrapped itself around the knight, and it seems he will have no chance of escape. Sir Prance-a-lot is a brave and skilled warrior, so perhaps he will defeat this wingless dragon yet.

Meanwhile, back inside the castle, a worried damsel is chained to a pillar. She is waiting for Sir Prance-a-lot to slay the dragon and rescue her. She does not have to wait long. Here comes the dashing knight to the rescue! How fortunate she is to have such a brave friend to save her from peril!

Identify things in the picture that do not match the story.

Name

Integrate Information

SEARCH FOR NESSIE

ADVENTURE #36 Join the hunt for the Loch Ness monster. Start your search at the library where investigative reporter Bea Sharp will help you find an encyclopedia entry and a poem about this creature.

Terror in Scotland

I've seen the fierce winged dragon
With mouth of flame and smoke
And dreamed of the elusive Sasquatch—
Still chasing me when I awoke.

I've ridden the great Greek Satyr
With body part man, part beast.
I've battled the monstrous Hydra
Who wore nine heads, at least!

I've flown on the grotesque Griffin—
Eagle head, lion body and tail.
I've come to face the Yeti,
And shuddered till I grew pale.

I've danced with a mighty Unicorn
(Now doesn't that sound absurd?)
I've escaped a deadly Siren—
A creature half woman, half bird.

But I've never shrieked in horror,
Never trembled and shook with dread.
I have never cried like a baby,
Nor stopped breathing like the dead.
No, I never knew sheer terror,
Not awake or asleep, I confess,
Until I saw, for a moment
The Monster of Loch Ness—
The massive
Rising
Grasping
Writhing
SERPENT
Of
Loch
Ness.

Loch Ness Monster

is a large animal that some people believe lives in Loch Ness, a large lake in Northern Scotland. There are hundreds of reported sightings. But if it does exist, it is hard to prove.

The creature is nicknamed Nessie. It is described as having a long, slim neck, flippers, and or two humps. Some believe it may be related to a dinosaur-like reptile or a present-day sea animal like the seal or manatee.

Sightings have been reported as far back as 565. In 1930, when a new highway made the lake more accessible, the sightings increased. People search the lake in boats or with diving equipment. In 1934, a doctor took a photo that shows a long, dinosaur-like neck and a head extending out of the water.

Since 1960, scientists have used sonar to explore Loch Ness. They have found large moving bodies in the lake, but do not agree on whether the sonar detected one big creature or a school of fish.

In 1972 and 1975, researchers from the Academy of Applied Science in Boston took underwater photos of what they claimed was the Loch Ness Monster. However, many experts question the value of these photos.

Whether or not Nessie is really there, she attracts thousands of tourists and searchers to Loch Ness each year. She also inspires the imagination of many children, adults, artists, and writers.

After you read the above information, follow the directions on the next page, page 68.

Use with page 68.

Name ____________________

What have you learned about the Loch Ness Monster from the two texts on page 67 (and the illustration on this page)?

Use this space to make a list of what you have learned. Be ready to use your list to share information about this topic in an essay, article, or speech.

Use with page 67.

Name

READING

FOUNDATIONAL SKILLS

Grade 4

BEACH BEHAVIOR

There's a bit of misbehavior at the beach today! What does *misbehavior* mean? The prefix *mis* changes the word *behavior* to a word that means "bad behavior."

A **prefix** changes the meaning of the root word in some way. Look at the meanings of the prefixes on the chart. Use these to write the meaning of each word below.

Meanings of Some Prefixes

a	(on)
anti	(against)
be	(make)
dis, im, un	(not)
inter	(between)
mid	(middle)
mini	(small)
mis	(bad, wrong)
multi	(many)
over	(too much)
pre	(before)
re	(again)
sub	(under, below)
trans	(across)
uni	(one)

Read each word and write its meaning.

1. unicycle ______________________
2. ashore______________________
3. befriend ______________________
4. subnormal ______________________
5. misspell ______________________
6. overpriced______________________
7. midfield ______________________
8. antiwar______________________
9. transatlantic ______________________
10. afoot______________________
11. rewrite ______________________
12. predawn ______________________
13. multicolored______________________
14. impossible ______________________
15. minivan ______________________
16. interstate ______________________
17. unfriendly ______________________
18. dishonest ______________________

Name ______________________

PERIL AT SEA

What will happen to the storm-tossed ship? These words will give you some clues to help you imagine what will happen.

Read each word. Choose at least ten. Write the meanings below the words.

Suffix	Meaning
en	(to make)
ful	(full of, like)
fy	(to cause to be)
ic	(like, pertaining to)
ism	(act or quality of)
less	(without)
lets	(small)
ment	(act or quality of)
ness	(state or condition of)
or	(one who)
ous	(full of, like)
ship	(state or quality of)
some	(full of)
ward	(toward)
y	(like, full of)

A **suffix** is a word part that can be added to the end of a word to change the word's meaning.

PERILOUS

EXCITEMENT

STORMY

FRIGHTEN

HARDSHIP

FEARFUL

ROCKY

HORRIFIC

NERVOUS

SEAWARD

HOPELESS

COURAGEOUS

SURVIVOR

DANGEROUS

TERRIFY

DROPLETS

SAILOR

LOSTNESS

HEROISM

TROUBLESOME

Name

UNFORGETTABLE!

When you come face-to-face with a weird sea creature, it is a truly unforgettable experience! The word *unforgettable* is built from the root word *forget.* Then other word parts (a prefix and a suffix) are added to the word. If you know your roots, you can read and create all kinds of words.

Choose the right root from the box to form each of the words described.

Root	Meaning
act	(act, do)
aqua	(water)
carn	(flesh)
dorm	(sleep)
dynam	(energy)
flam	(burn)
fug	(flee)
labor	(work)
mon	(warn)
phobia	(fear)
port	(carry)
scend	(climb)
tele	(far)
vis	(see)

1. ____________ivore — eater of flesh
2. zoo ____________ — fear of animals
3. ____________itive — one who flees
4. ad____________ition — warning
5. ____________ible — able to be seen
6. ____________tic — pertaining to water
7. ____________ion — the act of doing
8. ____________mable — easily burned
9. de ____________ — climb down
10. ____________ic — full of energy
11. ____________itory — place to sleep
12. ____________scope — instrument for seeing far
13. trans ____________ — carry across
14. ____________atory — place to work
15. arachna ____________ — fear of spiders
16. ____________able — able to be carried
17. phobo____________ — fear of fear
18. a ____________ — to climb up

Name

SUBMARINE WATCH

Root	Meaning
ann	(year)
aqua	(water)
ast	(star)
auto	(self)
bene	(good, well)
bio	(life)
cycl	(circle)
frag	(break)
geo	(earth)
graph	(write)
grav	(heavy)
labor	(work)
lib	(book)
loc	(place)
mar	(sea)
meter	(measure)
mini	(small)
mot, mov	(move)
ped	(foot)
pend	(hang)
port	(carry)
sol	(sun)
vac	(empty)
term	(end)

The submarine travels close to the bottom of the ocean. It's down there moving around among the roots! *Submarine* is a word that is formed from the root word *mar*, meaning "sea," and the prefix *sub* and suffix *ine*.

Read the roots and their meanings. Add a suffix or prefix (or both) to form 20 new words. Try to make at least 20 words!

Name

SHIPWRECK!

Diver Delbert was amazed to find a shipwreck loaded with words! Oddly enough, every one of these words could be part of a compound word, like the word *shipwreck*.

Using the words on the boat as one part of the compound, make as many compound words as you can. You can make a compound word by adding another word to the beginning or the end of one of these words. Use two words from the boat, or add other words not found here! Write the words you create in the middle of the page. If you need more space, use the back of the page.

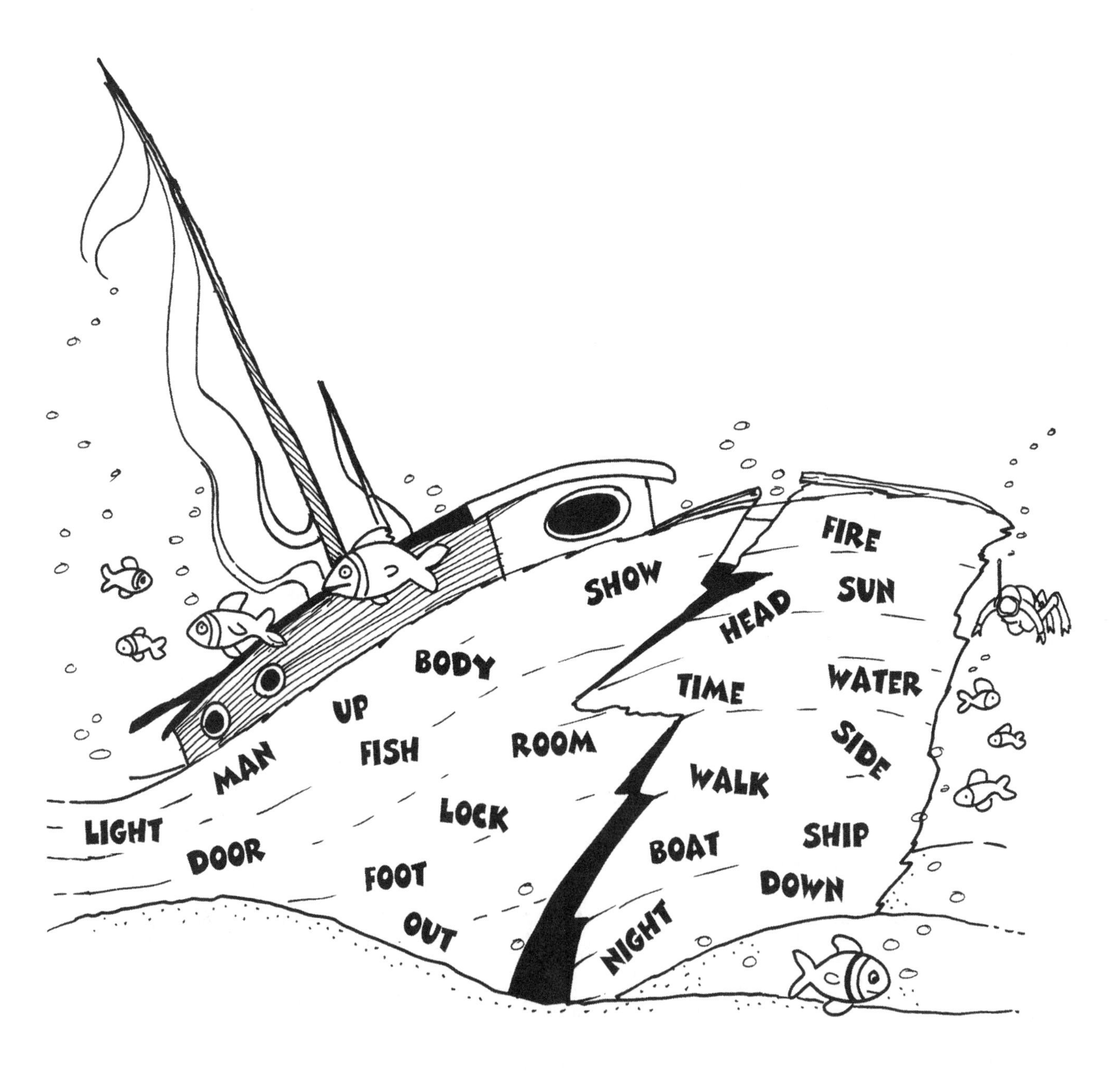

Name

THE WHOLE IN THE PALE

What's wrong with this title? It's a case of mixed-up homophones! What should it be?

Read about all the happenings on the beach today. Choose the correct word for the sentence. Write it in the blank.

1. Chester decided to ____________ (berry, bury) Angelina.
2. Who wants to run ____________ (straight, strait) into the ocean?
3. "You ____________ (through, threw) that too high!" hollered Josie.
4. "I ____________ (caught, cot) it anyway!"
5. Don't you think that the ____________ (sees, seize, seas) are pretty wild today?
6. That dead fish is giving off a very ____________ (foul, fowl) odor.
7. Don't trip over the ____________ (pale, pail)! You'll ____________ (brake, break) a leg!
8. Erwin went to the fishing ____________ (peer, pier) and caught six fish in one ____________ (hour, our).
9. Who ____________ (beet, beat) Oliver in the surfing contest?
10. Aunt Fannie ____________ (taught, taut) me how to build cool sand castles.
11. Let's ____________ (buy, by) ____________ (some, sum) cotton candy at the pier.
12. I can't! I only have twenty ____________ (cents, sense).
13. The hot sun is burning my ____________ (feet, feat).
14. Two squawking seagulls ____________ (flu, flew) toward my potato chips!
15. When the hurricane comes, the tourists will ____________ (flee, flea) from the beach.

Name ______________________________

WHAT YOU SEE IN THE SEA

What Ramón sees in the sea is a lot of fish with words! Curiously, both words on each fish sound the same.

Choose a pair of words to complete each sentence below. Write the correct word in the correct spot.

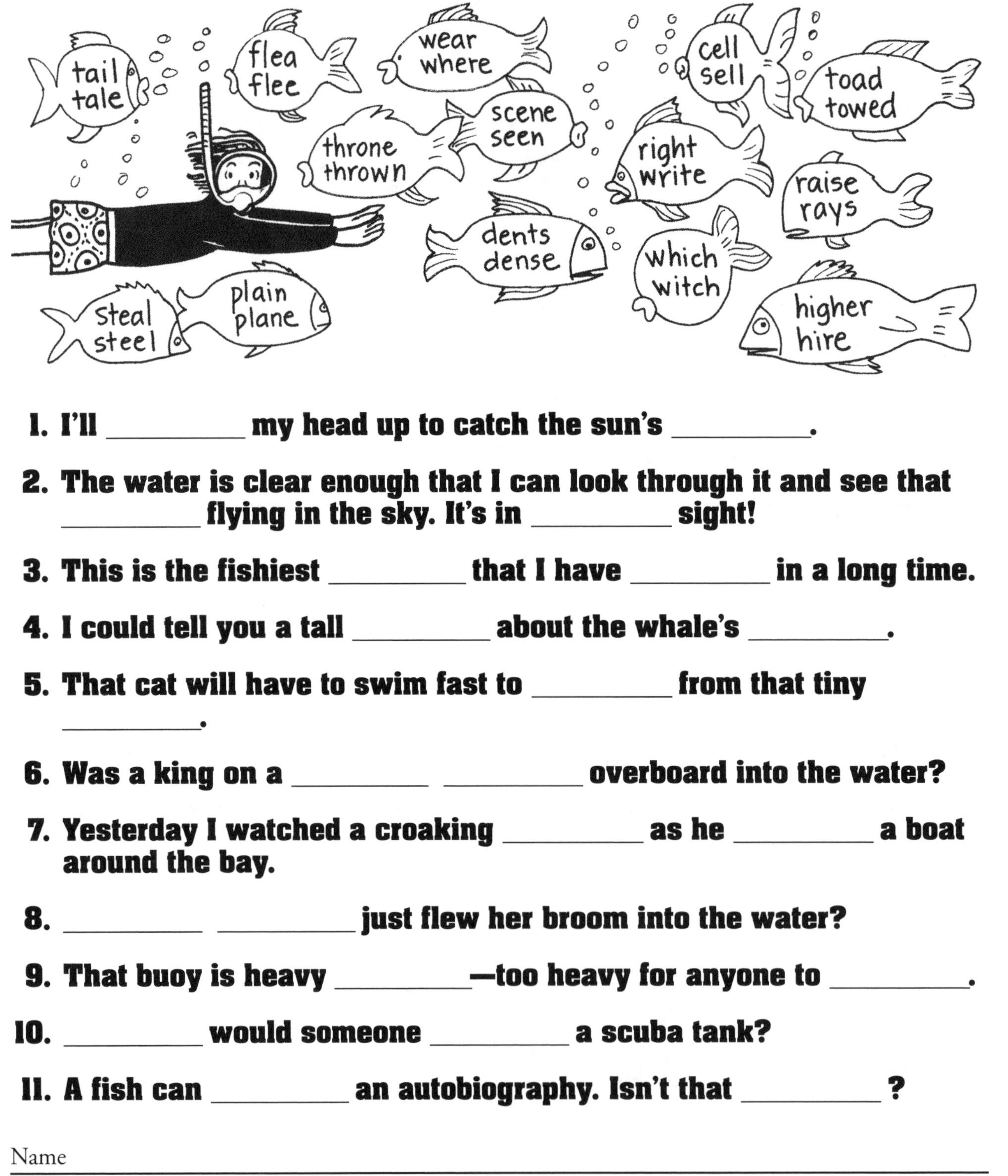

1. I'll _________ my head up to catch the sun's _________.

2. The water is clear enough that I can look through it and see that _________ flying in the sky. It's in _________ sight!

3. This is the fishiest _________ that I have _________ in a long time.

4. I could tell you a tall _________ about the whale's _________.

5. That cat will have to swim fast to _________ from that tiny _________.

6. Was a king on a _________ _________ overboard into the water?

7. Yesterday I watched a croaking _________ as he _________ a boat around the bay.

8. _________ _________ just flew her broom into the water?

9. That buoy is heavy _________—too heavy for anyone to _________.

10. _________ would someone _________ a scuba tank?

11. A fish can _________ an autobiography. Isn't that _________?

Name

WHERE WOULD YOU FIND THIS?

Fisherman Fred has found some very strange things in his net. Is that where they belong?

Decide where each one of these things would be found. Circle the correct choice.

Where would you find . . .

1. . . . **a narwhale**?
   a. at a computer
   b. in the ocean
   c. in a candy store

2. . . . **a chauffeur**?
   a. in a shoebox
   b. in a coffee cake
   c. driving a car

3. . . . **an almanac**?
   a. floating in a pool
   b. in a library
   c. acting on stage

4. . . . **a sundae**?
   a. in a hardware store
   b. on a menu
   c. talking on the phone

5. . . . **a molar**?
   a. making a movie
   b. in your mouth
   c. riding a motorcycle

6. . . . **a trombone**?
   a. in a bucket
   b. growing on a tree
   c. in an orchestra

7. . . . **a wrench**?
   a. on a sundae
   b. in a church
   c. in a toolbox

8. . . . **a sternum**?
   a. in your body
   b. singing in a choir
   c. in a dresser drawer

9. . . . **a mariner**?
   a. sailing a ship
   b. growing in a garden
   c. in a salad

10. . . . **a preview**?
    a. at a movie theater
    b. at a wedding
    c. snorkeling at a reef

11. . . . **an attorney**?
    a. in your bloodstream
    b. in your bank account
    c. in a courtroom

12. . . . **aqua socks**?
    a. on a snorkeler
    b. on a sandwich
    c. on the moon

13. . . . **an advertisement**?
    a. in a shell
    b. on a poster
    c. in a fishing boat

Name

Phonics, Word Recognition

WHERE WOULD YOU FIND THAT?

Fisherwoman Freeda has found some more weird stuff in her net. Is this where it belongs?

Decide where each of these would be found. Circle the correct choice or choices.

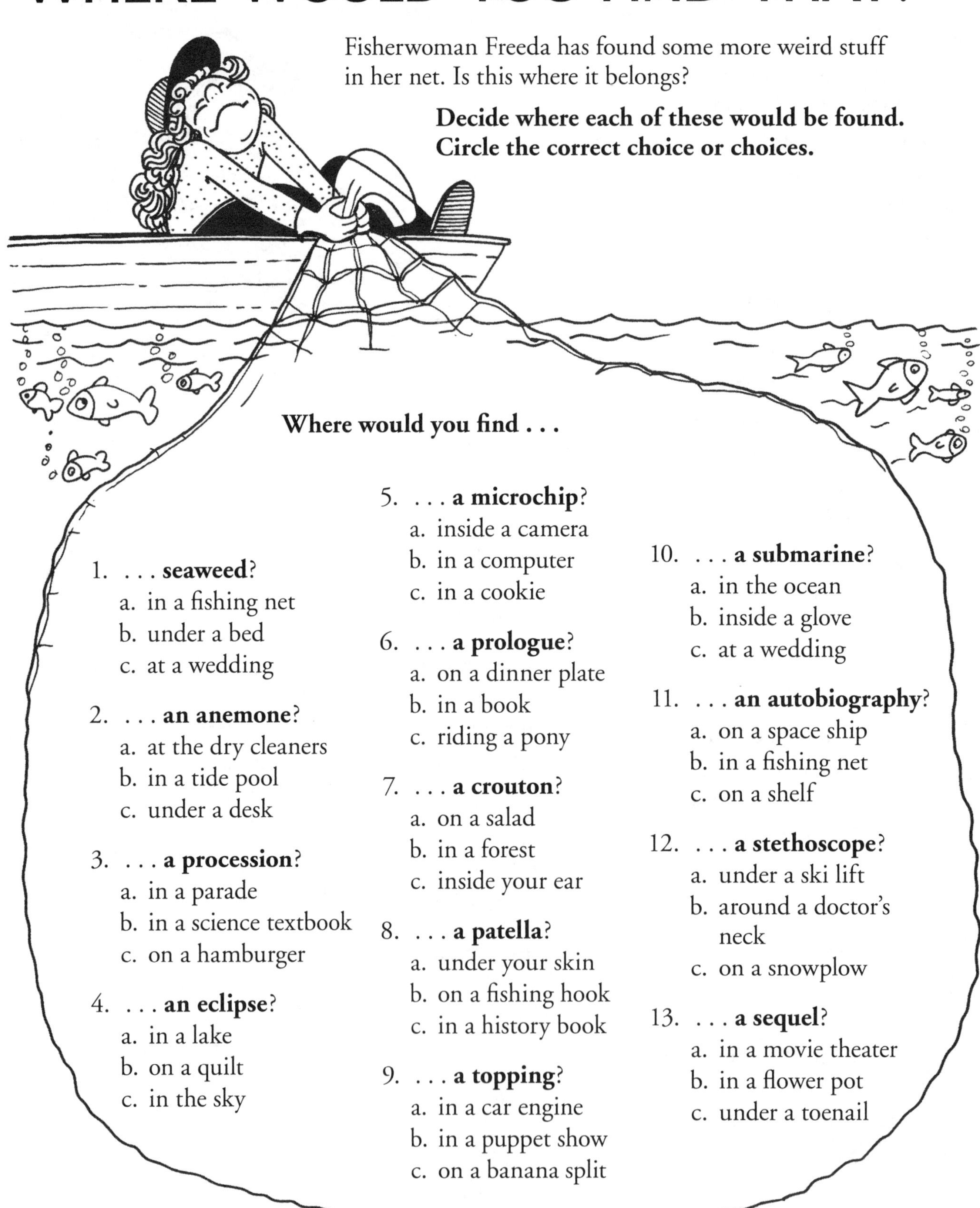

Where would you find . . .

1. . . . **seaweed**?
   a. in a fishing net
   b. under a bed
   c. at a wedding

2. . . . **an anemone**?
   a. at the dry cleaners
   b. in a tide pool
   c. under a desk

3. . . . **a procession**?
   a. in a parade
   b. in a science textbook
   c. on a hamburger

4. . . . **an eclipse**?
   a. in a lake
   b. on a quilt
   c. in the sky

5. . . . **a microchip**?
   a. inside a camera
   b. in a computer
   c. in a cookie

6. . . . **a prologue**?
   a. on a dinner plate
   b. in a book
   c. riding a pony

7. . . . **a crouton**?
   a. on a salad
   b. in a forest
   c. inside your ear

8. . . . **a patella**?
   a. under your skin
   b. on a fishing hook
   c. in a history book

9. . . . **a topping**?
   a. in a car engine
   b. in a puppet show
   c. on a banana split

10. . . . **a submarine**?
    a. in the ocean
    b. inside a glove
    c. at a wedding

11. . . . **an autobiography**?
    a. on a space ship
    b. in a fishing net
    c. on a shelf

12. . . . **a stethoscope**?
    a. under a ski lift
    b. around a doctor's neck
    c. on a snowplow

13. . . . **a sequel**?
    a. in a movie theater
    b. in a flower pot
    c. under a toenail

Name

WRITING

Grade 4

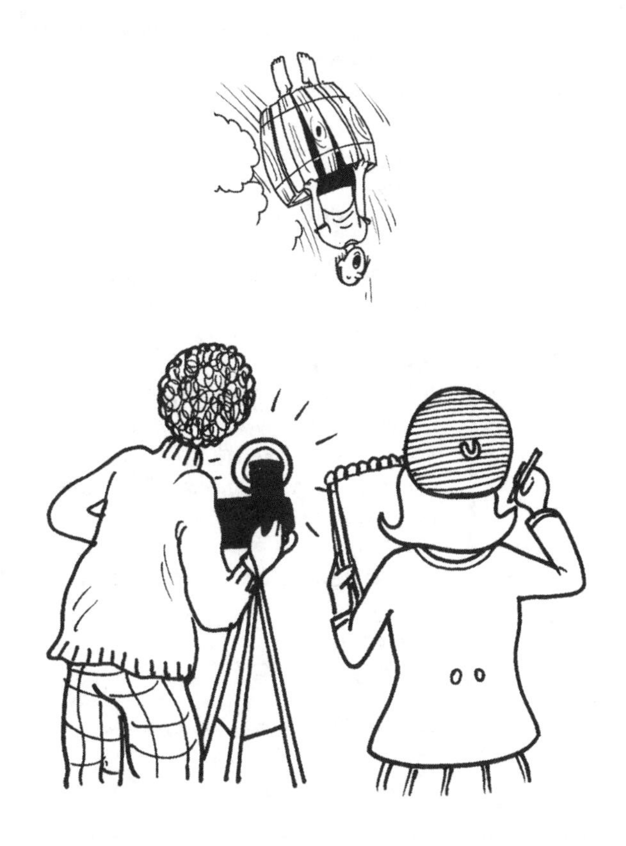

IN MY OPINION

A letter to the editor of a newspaper or magazine is a way for readers to express opinions. They comment on something that the magazine or newspaper has published. Or, they just express an opinion about any public matter.

Express your opinion in a letter to the editor. Follow the instructions on the next page (page 81).

Dear Editor,
I am shocked by your negative attitude about the new city tax on restaurant food. The tax is for a good cause—which you ignore.

Just a small amount added to each meal adds up to thousands of dollars for our city parks. This is good for the young people of our town. It gives us nice, clean places to play and relax. The soccer fields, softball fields, and swimming pool are used by children and adults alike. These parks provide safe, pleasant places for healthy family and physical activities.

All of our restaurants have good food. If I buy a $4 sandwich, it only costs 20¢ extra for the tax. Even with an expensive meal of $50, the 5% tax only adds $2.50. That's not bad! And with so many tourists buying meals, the money is not even coming out of our own pockets! The tourists benefit from our lovely town and parks too.

I certainly hope you will reconsider your biases about this tax.

Sincerely, Whitney

Dear Editor,
In your September issue, you had a great article about pushy snowboarders. I agree with your viewpoint.

I have had several unpleasant and dangerous experiences with boarders behaving carelessly.

Keep writing about this. Perhaps you will help get the ski hill to create a separate space for the snowboarders.

Yours truly,
Dionne

Dear Editor,
Your article about snowboarders was unfair and biased.

Most boarders are not careless. We follow the rules. We are citizens with rights. I wonder if you have ever even been to the mountain to see this for yourself.

Back off! Your claims are not true.

Sincerely,
Disgruntled

Dear Editor,

Everyone in this town is talking about year-round school. You have now written about it three times. But no one is talking to the kids!

The adults and town leaders have hearings and meetings. A special committee is making plans for a completely different school calendar. This makes me angry. Something is being planned that changes our whole lives—especially taking away most of our summer vacation. It is unfair to go ahead without including students in the decision. We have opinions too. We have important ideas. This is our education. We should be consulted.

Please use your influence to get kids in on the discussion.

Sincerely,
A Very Mad Kid

Use with page 81.

Name

Write a letter to the editor that gives your opinion. Use one of the ideas below, or write about any other idea.

Introduce the topic. Give your opinion. Give reasons for your opinion. Write a clear ending.

Use with page 80.

Name

Text Types, Opinion

CONVINCE ME!

Murphy wrote this jingle for MBG (Mystery Bubble Gum). Since it was aired on TV three months ago, the sales of MBG have tripled. (A jingle is a catchy advertising ad or slogan—often set to music.)

Write a jingle for each of these products. Or name your own product and write a jingle on the back of the paper. A jingle must convince buyers to try the product.

MBG is the bubblegum for me
I don't care if it's got broccoli!

Carrots, peas, and berries
Onions, beans, and cherries
It's got fruits galore
And veggies twenty-four.

We buy packs by the dozen.
I share them with my cousin.
I love to chew and pop it.
No vitamin can stop it.

I don't care if it's got broccoli
'Cause MBG is the bubblegum for me!

Write a paragraph, poem, advertisement, or song that could convince someone to **do** one of these things. (Or you may choose something else!)

- ... try eating chocolate-covered ants
- ... learn to use the Internet
- ... take a trip to the Bermuda Triangle
- ... buy organic food
- ... learn to ride a wild bull
- ... never get a tattoo
- ... search for Bigfoot in a deep forest
- ... ride an upside-down roller coaster
- ... go to summer school

tuna-artichoke ice cream

a parrot hat

try eating chocolate-covered ants

Name

TERRIBLE CHOICES

Butterfly hunting in Quicksand Swamp is probably a "no-no."

There are great places to take a vacation, and there are some not-so-great places! Of course, people have different ideas about this.

Choose a place that would be a terrible choice for a vacation. It can be real or fictitious. Give the name of the place. Tell what to bring, and how to survive while there. Make sure your writing has a beginning, middle, and end.

I. ______________________________

A. ______________________________

B. ______________________________

C. ______________________________

II. ______________________________

A. ______________________________

B. ______________________________

C. ______________________________

III. ______________________________

A. ______________________________

B. ______________________________

C. ______________________________

IV. ______________________________

A. ______________________________

B. ______________________________

C. ______________________________

Name

HERE'S HOW

Just about everybody loves a good milkshake. Just about everybody can make a milkshake. Here's a chance for you to share your best milkshake recipe!

List the ingredients and supplies. Then write a paragraph that describes exactly how to make the milkshake so that it turns out just right!

Name

THE TALLEST OF TALES

FROSTBITE in MONTANA

How cold is cold? Do you think you have ever really been cold? Well, listen to this, and then you can decide. Last winter I went to Montana to visit my Uncle Fred. He told me to bring warm clothes. Was I ever glad that I did! The first morning that I was there, it was so cold that the chickens laid frozen eggs and the cows gave ice cream instead of milk. My words froze as I spoke them and dropped right to the ground and shattered. The dog's shadow froze on the ground the minute he stepped out of the house. Uncle Fred said that shadow did not thaw until April. Well, that's the last time I'll visit Montana in the winter. Uncle Fred says to come in August. He wants me to see the chicken lay scrambled eggs from the terrible heat.

WANTED: The tallest tale in the county!
It's time for the Tall Tale Contest again. SPARK magazine is waiting for its readers to send in tall tales this year.

REQUIREMENTS: The tale **must** have facts or details that show great exaggeration. These must be things that could not possibly be true! This is one place where lies are okay! In fact, the bigger the lies, the better the tale!

Would you like to enter the contest? Choose a topic that is a good one for exaggeration. Then write a tale and polish it until it is ready to send in to the magazine. Make sure your tale has: a good title
a smashing beginning
a solid middle
a great ending
Good luck! Maybe you'll win a tall, tall prize!

Start your Tall Tale here:

Name

HE SAID . . . SHE SAID

In a cartoon, the dialogue can be shown in talk balloons. (*Dialogue* is the conversation between two or more characters.) In a story, dialogue is shown with quotation marks and other punctuation.

Write a story that includes the dialogue found in one of these cartoons. Follow the directions on the next page (page 87).

Use with page 87.

Name

Choose one of the cartoons from page 86. Create a story that includes the dialogue in that cartoon. Give the story a captivating beginning. Tell what happens. Give the story a good ending. Use as much dialogue as you wish. Use correct punctuation for the dialogue.

Draw another cartoon to match part of the story.

Use with page 86.

Name

QUITE BY ACCIDENT

Murphy was in such a hurry to get this accident report written that she got it all mixed up. Can you straighten it out before it goes to press?

When I arrived, I found Farmer McCully's pigs looking shocked. No one was hurt, not even the pigs. Farmer McCully called 911 at noon to report a loud roaring sound that was shaking the earth near his farm. Just then, I heard terrible screaming in addition to the loud roaring sound. Unbelievably, a bathtub was whirling through the air. I was in the area, so I raced to the farm. I looked up in the sky toward the terrible noise. Fortunately, the tub landed safely in the pig pen. A young man in the tub was screaming for his life.

Rewrite this report to match the actual happenings of the scene. Give it a good beginning and ending. Describe the event.

Name

WORDS ON THE MOVE

The words just don't seem to want to sit still on the page today! They keep winding and moving all over. Murphy, the magazine editor, is preparing a page with writing that looks as if it were painted on the page instead of written in nice, neat lines. You could call this painted writing!

Read the page. Then choose one of the ideas from the Idea File, and try some painted writing of your own. Use another piece of paper.

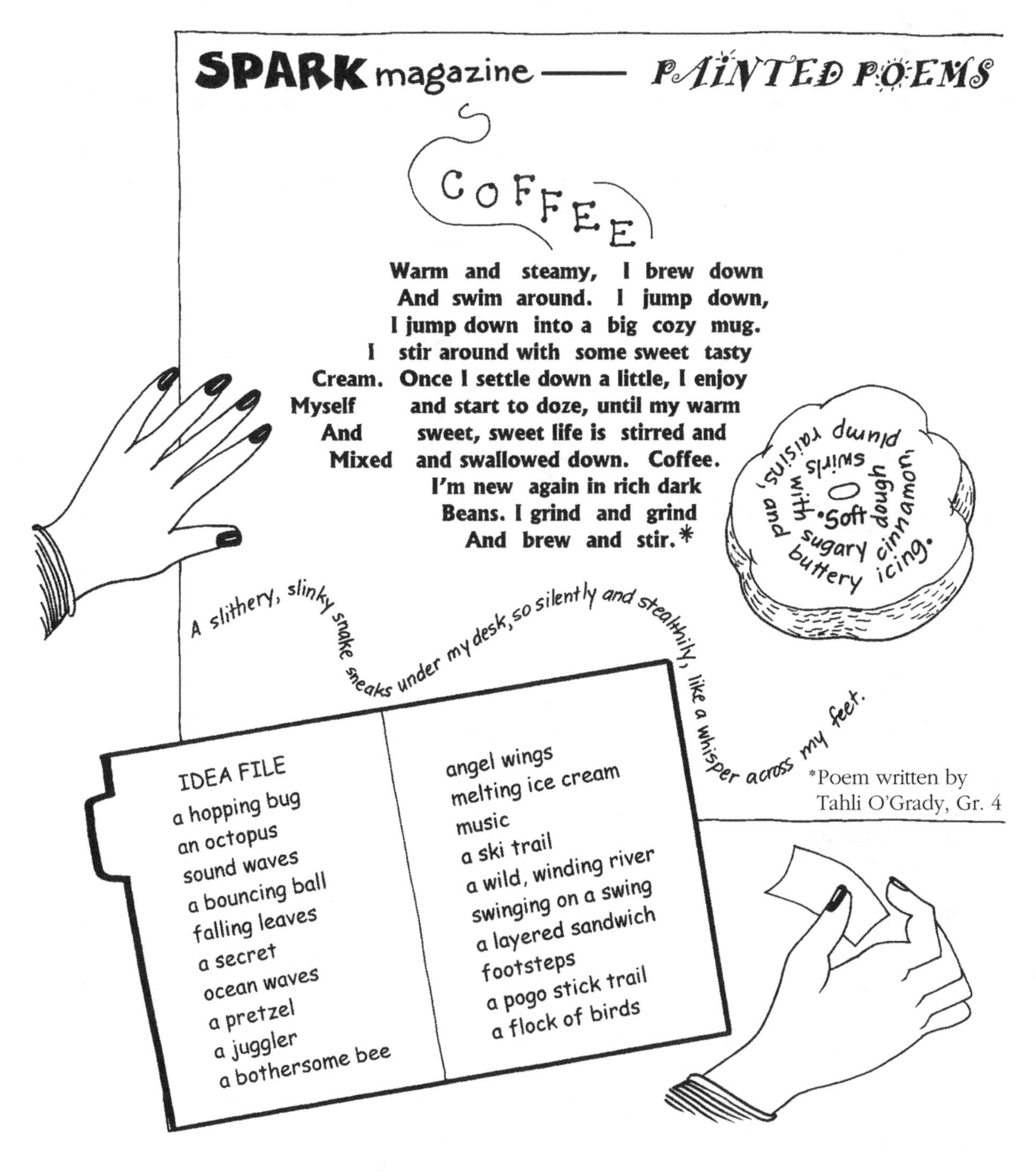

Name

ASK ME ANYTHING!

If you want to find out something, you need to ask the right questions. Good reporters ask good questions. They plan their questions before they go investigating, so that they will know exactly what to ask.

Think about the questions you would ask to find out interesting information about the people or events on pages 90 and 91. Get ready for some interviews by writing down the questions. Write clear, complete questions that ask exactly what you want to know! Write at least four good questions to ask each person.

1. ***a lion tamer*** ______________________________

____

____

____

2. ***a world record-holder*** ______________________________

BUZZ
BUZZ
BUZZZ

____

____

____

3. ***a high school student*** ______________________________

____

____

____

Use with page 91.

Name

Produce Writing

**Get ready for some interviews by writing down the questions.
Write clear, complete questions that ask exactly what you want to know.**

Use with page 90.

Name

PICTURE THIS

Keanu is a news photographer. He follows reporters around and gets the pictures to back up the stories. At the end of the day yesterday, some of his photos were lost. Interestingly, the reporter also lost one of her written pieces!

Where the photo is missing, read the article and re-create the picture. Where the writing is missing, write an article, poem, essay, story, or opinion to match the ideas shown in the picture.

1.

Sharks have come to our beaches! Lifeguards and swimmers have reported many sightings of sharks close to shore at the beaches south of the city. One surfer reported a very close call. A shark actually took a huge bite out of his board! Sharks rarely come into the swimming area or bother swimmers. Officials have closed the beaches to swimmers until further notice—and until the sharks move on to deeper waters!

2.

Name

FEATURE YOURSELF

Polish up your memory! Search into your past! Think about your future! Then get ready to write an article that features yourself!

Finish these phrases to collect information about yourself in the past, present, and future. Then use the space on the next page (page 95) to organize your ideas for writing.

About Myself

1. When I was little, I was afraid of ____________________

   Now, I'm afraid of ____________________

2. Something I would never want to do is ____________________
3. I am very good at ____________________
4. Nothing makes me madder than ____________________
5. The most important thing to me is ____________________
6. My most embarrassing experience was ____________________
7. Something I will never do again is ____________________
8. Not long ago, I ____________________
9. Something I want to learn is ____________________
10. Some day, I hope to ____________________
11. I am most proud of ____________________
12. Last year, I ____________________
13. The hardest thing I've learned is ____________________
14. If I could change the world, I would ____________________

Use with page 94.

Name ____________________

Create categories or main ideas from the information on page 93 for three paragraphs.

Write notes and numbers of ideas from page 93 that fit into each category. Add other ideas if you wish.

Add notes and ideas that you will use for an opening paragraph and for a closing paragraph.

Here's something I hope never to do again—eat a bowl of escamoles!

Escamoles are the eggs of the giant black Liometopum ant!

Notes for Opening

Paragraph 1

(Topic)

Paragraph 2

(Topic)

Paragraph 3

(Topic)

Notes for Conclusion

Use with page 93.

Name

STRAIGHT FROM THE PAGES

Stories are full of enticing characters, fascinating settings, surprising events, and great drama. Search a story (a short story, novel, or play) to find how the author presents these details!

Select a play or story. Choose a character, a setting, or an event from the story. Write a description that gives a clear picture of that character, setting, or event. Use details from the story.

Name

EVIDENCE, PLEASE!

Information is everywhere you look! Books, magazines, DVD's, the Internet, newspapers, apps on all kinds of devices—all are places you can go to learn just about anything! Take a close-up look at a presentation of information.

Select a sample of informational text. Choose a main point the author makes. Find evidence or reasons that the author uses to support the point. Describe the evidence in a paragraph.

Title and source of text________________________________

A main point is______________________________________

Evidence

Evidence

How to Feed an Alligator

The Bermuda Triangle Fact or Fiction

Black Holes—What Are They?

Name

LANGUAGE

Grade 4

RELATIVELY SPEAKING

Cousins Francie and Flossie love being relatives. The sentences on the tennis court include some other relatives—relative pronouns and adverbs. These words are used to link one part of the sentence to another part or to another word. They have the job of showing how one part is related to the other. (Examples are: *that, which, whom, who, whichever, whomever, whoever, whose, when, where, why.*)

Underline each relative adverb.
Circle the two parts of the sentence that it links.

1. The town where they live has twelve tennis courts.
2. Today is the day when they will start the tournament.
3. This is the court where they play most often.
4. Francie can't understand why Flossie beat her!

Circle the correct relative pronoun for the sentence.

5. Francie is the cousin (who, whom) won the first game.
6. She loves to challenge (whomever, whoever) will play.
7. (Whichever, Which) cousin wins buys the other a milkshake.
8. The game (that, whatever) started before lunch was rained out.
9. Someone stepped on that water bottle, (whichever, which) was empty.
10. Is that player (whom, who) you beat another cousin?
11. It was her brother (whom, whose) racquet broke.

Name

OUT OF THE PAST

Meet Sir Felix Frog, an actor playing a knight right out of the Middle Ages. Sir Felix is always in the middle of some action! Progressive verbs are good for writing about Felix—because a progressive verb describes an ongoing action! (Progressive verbs use *am, is, are, was, were, will be,* or *shall be* with the *ing* form of a verb.)

Read the sentences about Felix's activities. Do the verbs show ongoing action? If NOT, mark the sentence with an X. Then write a verb in progressive form.

___ 1. Sir Felix is fighting a dragon today. ____________________

___ 2. "I conquered the foe!" he bragged. ____________________

___ 3. Yesterday, he fought more! ____________________

___ 4. Tomorrow the dragon will be taking the day off. ____________________

___ 5. Will Felix go to the dungeon? ____________________

___ 6. He could have stopped that dragon! ____________________

___ 7. The dragons are getting fiercer. ____________________

___ 8. Were they breathing fire? ____________________

___ 9. Dragon breath will have burned the castle. ____________________

___ 10. Did he rescue any damsels in distress this morning? ____________________

___ 11. No, he was having breakfast. ____________________

___ 12. People will be remembering Felix as a great actor. ____________________

Name ____________________

TWO TO LEAP

The mischievous frog twins love a good game of leapfrog. Practice good grammar while you watch them jump.

Each item (1 to 10) gives a statement. Pay attention to the meaning of the statement. Choose the sentence below it that has the same meaning.

1. Do I have permission to jump?
   a. *May I jump now?*
   b. *Can I jump now?*

2. Freddie is required to count.
   a. *Freddie may count.*
   b. *Freddie must count.*

3. A frog is able to catch flies.
   a. *A frog may catch flies.*
   b. *A frog can catch flies.*

4. I'd advise them to take a rest.
   a. *They should take a rest.*
   b. *They could take a rest.*

5. It is possible that Frieda will stop for lunch.
   a. *Frieda might stop for lunch.*
   b. *Frieda would stop for lunch.*

6. It is necessary for the frogs to eat.
   a. *The frogs could eat.*
   b. *The frogs must eat.*

7. Are you able to play leapfrog?
   a. *May you play leapfrog?*
   b. *Can you play leapfrog?*

8. Is it possible for her to break a leg?
   a. *Could she break a leg?*
   b. *Would she break a leg?*

9. It is a good idea to be careful.
   a. *You ought to be careful.*
   b. *You might be careful.*

10. It is necessary for the game to end.
    a. *The game might end.*
    b. *The game must end.*

Name

ORDER, PLEASE!

There is plenty of disorder in the Frog family today! There are lots of wild little green frogs to manage. Here are some of the things the babysitter, Frieda, is trying to control.

Read the list. The adjectives are not in the best order. See the box above for a review of the best order for adjectives. Write each phrase in a better order.

Adjective Order	Examples
opinion	fun, smart
size	big, small
shape	circular, oblong
condition	fresh, wrinkled
color	red, orange
origin	French, English
material	silver, cotton

1. one two-year old smart nephew ______________________
2. a yellow rotten apple ______________________
3. a round toy broken sword ______________________
4. two plastic small cracked bottles ______________________
5. a sassy tiny baby ______________________
6. a square Chinese expensive plate ______________________

7. a silk red fancy scarf ______________________
8. a leather brown chair ______________________
9. some new terrible screams ______________________
10. one teenage frazzled babysitter ______________________

Name ______________________

PHRASES WITH CHARACTER

How would you describe the behavior or looks of these extraordinary characters? Use your skill with prepositional phrases to tell something about each of them.

Write two different prepositional phrases that somehow relate to each of the characters. Circle the preposition in each phrase. See the box below for some prepositions.

1. ______________________________
____

2. ______________________________
____

3. ______________________________
____

4. ______________________________
____

above	before	during	of	toward
about	behind	except	on	under
across	below	from	out of	until
after	beneath	in	outside	up
against	beside	inside	over	upon
among	between	into	since	with
around	by	like	through	within
as	despite	near	to	without

Name

WORDS THAT MAKE YOU LAUGH AND CRY

Some words make Frankie laugh. Others make him cry. Once he gets started laughing or crying, it's hard to get him to stop!

Frankie used some of these words in sentences. But sadly, these sentences are not complete, or are run-on sentences. Insert words or punctuation and fix capitalization to make complete sentences.

1. Can't stop giggling from all this tickling!

2. There's so much silliness these are the funniest jokes ever!

3. Whenever I see a hilarious comedy.

4. That's an absurd idea doesn't it give you the giggles?

5. Without laughter and humor.

6. Teasing me all the time.

7. All the insults are scary they make me feel lonely.

8. Terror from a dangerous adventure.

9. Feeling sorrow and feeling I want to whine.

Name

LOOK-ALIKE WORDS

Is Freddy, the hot air balloonist, checking out his **attitude** or his **altitude**? He needs to know the difference between the two words in order to be sure!

In each cloud, there is a word that looks a lot like another word. Sometimes the word is used correctly. Sometimes it is not. Color the clouds that show correct use of all words.

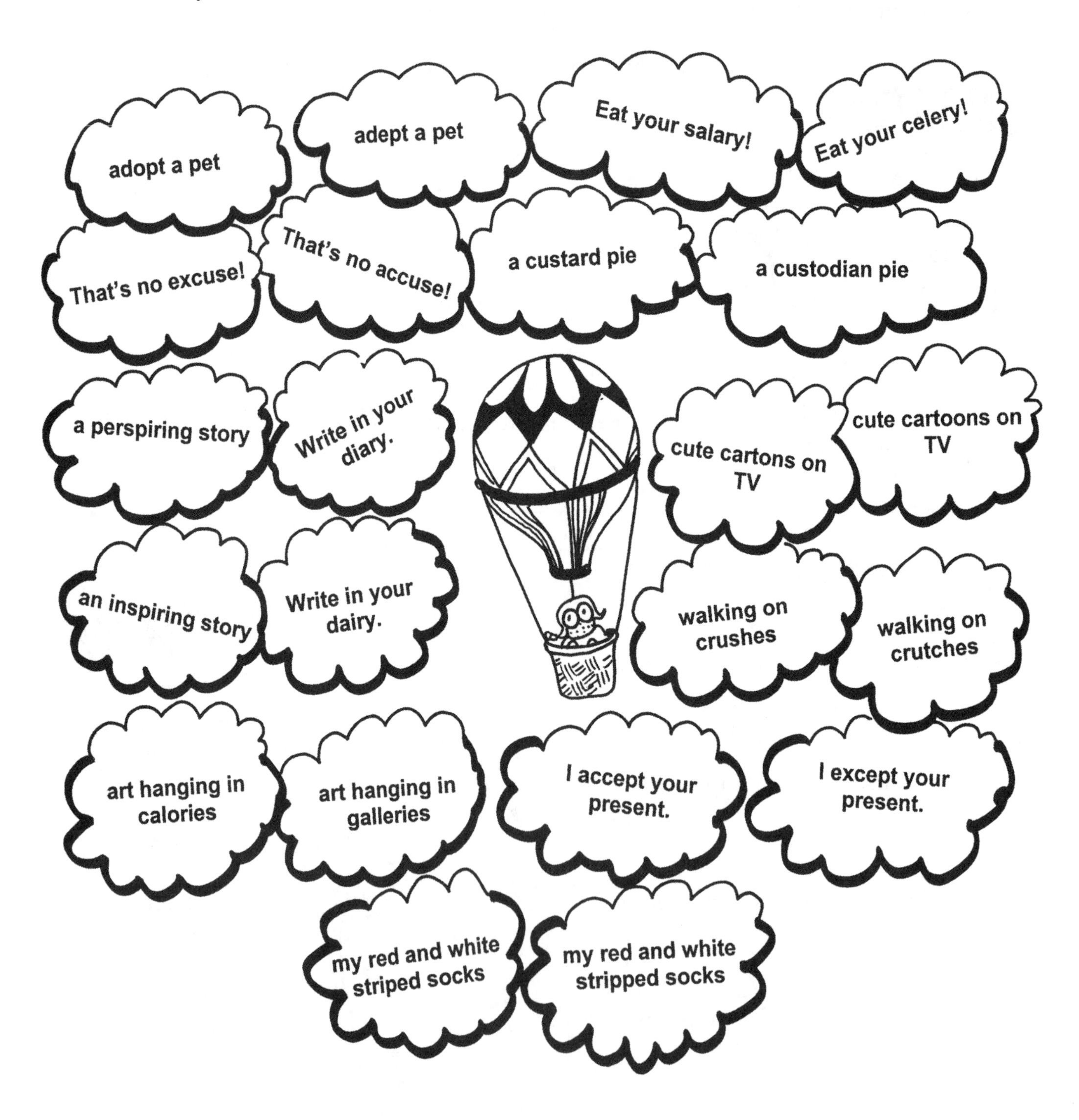

Name

TAKE A CLOSE LOOK

Fred can't quite get his binoculars adjusted. He's seeing some things that do not look right. Help him get things into clear focus.

Fix any capitalization mistakes within Fred's view. That way when he gets the binoculars in focus, everything he sees will be correct.

1. Welcome to the rio grande river!
2. drink coca cola!
3. **monday, september 1**
4. I love french Fries.
5. john f. kennedy, jr.

6. MY favorite book is the thirteenth gorilla.
7. **what's your favorite?**
8. is there really a prince charming?
9. **Read the declaration of independence.**
10. **I'll stop at target for some kleenex.**
11. **Visit the f.b.i. in washington, d.c.**
12. **Is there a mrs. easter bunny?**
13. omaha chamber of commerce
14. **let's read the story, "Marooned."**
15. **I learned spanish in costa rica.**
16. *sir frederick is my Cousin.*
17. **Happy st. patrick's day!**

Name

A GOOD TRICK

Manifrog the Magnificent is the most respected frog magician in the land. He pulls some amazing things out of his hat. Today he is pulling just the right punctuation marks needed for these sentences.

Look for missing punctuation.
Insert the right marks in the right spots!

1. A voice shouted, Introducing Manifrog the Magnificent
2. The room went dark for the show was about to begin.
3. A frog appeared but only his hat was visible.
4. Ladies and Gentlemen he said.
5. A light flashed and the hat exploded.
6. It rained commas or were those quotation marks?
7. Now I will turn these into rabbits he announced.
8. We could not see the black rabbits so he turned them red.
9. He asked Shall I turn them into doves
10. Manifrog waved his wand and off flew ten doves

Name

WHO'S GONE WRONG?

Sheriff Wilbur Wise Walfrog has just posted the pictures of all the scoundrels WANTED in Frogville. He has brought them into the station. They have all given their excuses.

Read each culprit's excuse. Sheriff Walfrog had some trouble writing their statements. Fix the errors in punctuation and capitalization.

William Weightlifter

Wretched Ray

Worst Woodpecker

Weird Wanda Worm

Wrestler Rachael

Weekend Warrior

"**William** insisted that window was already broken!"

"Furthermore he said" I was at the gym lifting weights.

Ray sweated "and mumbled I thought they were flies, not jewels".

Worst kept asking what bank? "I didn't see any bank."

I was never there said **Wanda**.

Wanda kept saying "I was never there"!

I did not squeeze that ice cream man; "I just hugged him insisted **Rachael**."

Weekend Warrior repeated I was riding my bike in China."

Name ______________________________

WORDS THAT CONFUSE

Cassie is confused about the spelling of these words.
Maybe it's because they are words that are often spelled wrong!

Help him out of his confusion. Find the correct spelling for each word. Circle it.

1. busness
   buziness
   business
   busyness

2. twelth
   twelvth
   twelfth
   twelveth

3. surprise
   suprize
   surprice
   surprise

4. cafateria
   cafetaria
   cafeteria
   cafeterria

5. calandar
   calendar
   calender
   calander

6. balloon
   baloon
   ballon
   baloone

7. embarrass
   embarass
   embbaras
   emmbarass

8. lisense
   lisence
   license
   licence

9. memary
   memory
   memry
   memmory

10. bannana
    bananna
    bannanna
    banana

11. memarise
    memorize
    memorise
    memmorize

12. nesessary
    nessessary
    necessary
    nessecary

13. Flordia
    Florida
    Floirda
    Floirida

14. restrant
    resturant
    restaurant
    restaurent

15. marshmellow
    marshmalow
    marshmallow
    marshmelow

16. reconize
    reconise
    recognize
    recognise

17. receive
    recieve
    resieve
    reseive

18. advertisement
    advertizment
    advertisment
    advertizement

19. trubble
    troubble
    troble
    trouble

20. vegtable
    vejetable
    veggetable
    vegetable

Name

SNIFFING OUT MISTAKES

Garth, the garbage collector, follows his nose to locate the garbage cans that need emptying. He is very good at deciding which ones have leftovers and other unwanted trash.

Which cans have unwanted misspelled words in them? Use your spelling sense to figure it out. Color the cans that have one or more misspelled words. Write the number of wrong words on the lid of each can (0–5).

Name

Conventions, Spelling

SIGNS FOR SPELLERS

Freida is surprised by all the signs on the beach. For one thing, they are rather hard to read because of all the errors.

Fix the signs. Rewrite the message on each sign.
Spell every word correctly!

Name

HEADLINES IN NEED OF HELP

The newspaper editor fell asleep at his desk this morning, so no one got rid of the spelling errors.

Edit these headlines. Write each one correctly in the space below the headline.

1. BURGLER STEELS PRESIOUS PAINTINGS

2. VOLCANOE CAUZES TERIBBLE TRADGEDY

3. GIANT SLEEPS TWO HUNDERD YEARS

4. ZOOKEEPER CHASES HIPOPOTOMOS TO MICHAGAN

5. MAGIGIUN PULLS NINTY RABITTS FROM HAT

6. PELICAN RESKUES CHILD FROM SINKING YAHT

7. WRESSTLER WINS MILLYUN DOLLER PRISE

8. DOCTER DISKOVERS MIRACAL CURE FOR WARTS

Name

IN PURSUIT OF THE BEST WORDS

Detective Sherlock Frog is searching for good words and phrases. He wants to find effective, interesting, precise writing.

Help him with his search. Circle the sentence in each pair that expresses the idea most precisely or effectively.

1. a. It was a rough trail.
   b. It was a treacherous trail.

2. a. A sleepwalker stumbled around the yard.
   b. A sleepwalker walked around the yard.

3. a. She held the coin in her hand.
   b. The coin was clenched in her tight fingers.

4. a. Isn't that a rickety, battered car?
   b. Isn't that such a beat-up old car?

5. a. That shark sneered as it passed by.
   b. That shark seems to be smiling.

6. a. An icy January wind bit my nose.
   b. The January wind felt cold and icy.

7. a. That waiter was grumpy.
   b. That waiter had a vinegary attitude.

8. a. Dark clouds poured out heavy raindrops.
   b. Angry clouds threw tantrums and sputtered water.

9. a. Buttery popcorn air caressed my nose.
   b. Warm popcorn air floated through the house.

10. a. The hilltop was covered in purple shadows.
    b. Fuzzy shadows purpled the hilltop.

Name

WHAT A THRILL!

The exclamation point at the end of the title adds punch to the title. It lets you know that this adventure is very exciting. It lets you know the frogs are doing something a bit beyond the ordinary.

Look at the punctuation in each sentence. Answer the question about what a punctuation mark does for the sentence.

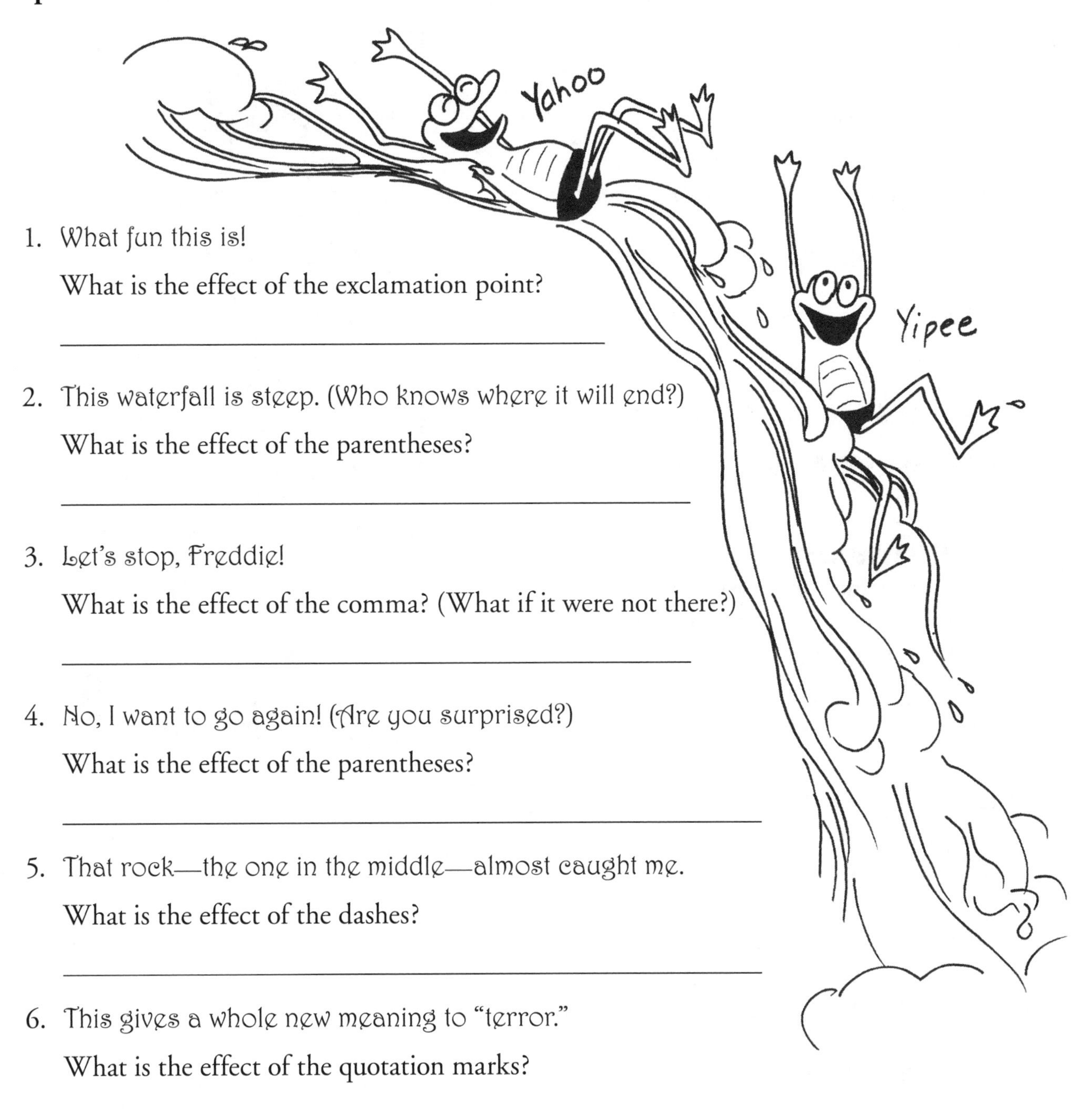

1. What fun this is!
   What is the effect of the exclamation point?
   ____

2. This waterfall is steep. (Who knows where it will end?)
   What is the effect of the parentheses?
   ____

3. Let's stop, Freddie!
   What is the effect of the comma? (What if it were not there?)
   ____

4. No, I want to go again! (Are you surprised?)
   What is the effect of the parentheses?
   ____

5. That rock—the one in the middle—almost caught me.
   What is the effect of the dashes?
   ____

6. This gives a whole new meaning to "terror."
   What is the effect of the quotation marks?
   ____

Name ______________________________

HOW DO WE TALK?

Professor Froglegs has written some different phrases on the board. He has asked his students to consider this question for each phrase or sentence: Where would you talk like this?

We use language a bit differently in formal situations than we do in informal situations. Read each phrase or sentence on the board.

1. Hey, how ya doin?
2. Please enter quietly.
3. Thank you, ladies and gentlemen, for coming.
4. Let's race to the door!
5. No way!
6. The key to this idea is the right vocabulary.

Tell whether it might be used in a formal or informal setting (circle one). Give an example of the setting.

1. **formal informal** ______________________________ *(example)*
2. **formal informal** ______________________________ *(example)*
3. **formal informal** ______________________________ *(example)*
4. **formal informal** ______________________________ *(example)*
5. **formal informal** ______________________________ *(example)*
6. **formal informal** ______________________________ *(example)*

Name ______________________________

SOUND-ALIKE WORDS

Does the music sound suite or sweet?
Are they singing a ballad or a ballot?
At the end of the performance, will the singers take a bough or a bow?

Watch out for words that sound alike (homonyms)! Don't get the wrong word for the wrong spot!

There are one or two words in each sentence that are wrong in the context. Circle those words. On the line, write the correct words for the context.

1. Who pride open this can of fudge? ______________________
2. Are your bones getting old and creeky? ______________________
3. I can't weight to see who wins the gold metal! ______________________
4. The king decided to leave his thrown after he had rained for forty years. ______________________
5. Mom scent her away from the table because she choose her food too loudly. ______________________
6. "Stay indoors tonight," Mother Rat warned her children. "You don't want to frees your tales!" ______________________
7. My ant's boss gave her a 10 percent rays. ______________________
8. Oh no! My library books have been overdo for a weak! ______________________
9. After the concert, all the singers' voices were a little horse. ______________________
10. My dog let out a hoop when he caught the cent of the skunk. ______________________
11. Instead of milk and cookies, I left milk and serial for Santa Claws. ______________________
12. Petal your bike hard, or you'll get to school after the bell has wrung. ______________________
13. The fleece are bothering our dog. Maybe we should cut off his hare. ______________________

Name ____

WORDS YOU CAN EAT

Famous Chef Pierre LaFrog serves wonderful delights at his Chez Froggie Café. Frogs who come there to dine can choose from several menus.

Read the menus carefully. One word is BOLD on each menu. (Number 4 has two bold words.) Use the menu and the idea of food to think about what the word means. Write a brief definition near the menu.

Name

DAISY'S DAFFY DAYS

Daisy loves to write in her diary. The last few days have been quite eventful! Read about her surprising experiences.

Notice the bold word in each diary entry. Use the context to decide what the word means. Write the meaning on the lines.

Friday, June 13

After today, my desire for celery has **waned**. I was laughing at the circus today—while I munched on celery. All those strings stuck in my throat, and I was rushed to the emergency room. They pulled it out. My throat is sore!

____

____

____

Saturday, June 14

Today, I got dragged into court! I was painting my fingernails on the bus. Someone reported me for spreading **noxious** fumes. The judge fined me for putting people's health at risk.

____

____

____

Sunday, June 15

Two **ghastly** ghosts crashed my birthday party. They were so creepy that all the kids hid. The ghosts ate all the birthday cake and ice cream.

____

____

____

Monday, June 16

I got so busy exercising today, that I forgot about school. After 553 push-ups, I remembered. The teacher gave me a large clock to help me be **punctual** in the future.

____

____

____

Tuesday, June 17

It's unbelievable—but I got caught in a **cyclone** today! With my bike and my dog, I was whirled around, picked up, and tossed to the next county by a wild wind.

____

____

____

Name ______________________________

AT THE ROOT OF IT ALL

It's good to get to the root of words! If you know root meanings, you can figure out the meanings of many words.

Use your knowledge of roots to write a meaning for each word.

1. supernatural

____

2. counterattack

____

3. annual

____

4. flammable

____

5. pedestrian

____

6. autograph

____

7. junction

____

8. decagon

____

9. acrophobia

____

10. monochrome

____

11. aquatic

____

12. cardiac

____

Name ______________________

ADD-IT-ON

These frogmen make use of prefixes to change the meanings of words. (Thousands of words have prefixes added to their beginnings.)

You might guess that their favorite prefix means "under"!

Use your knowledge of prefixes to find the right one for each bubble. The clues below give the meaning of the word.

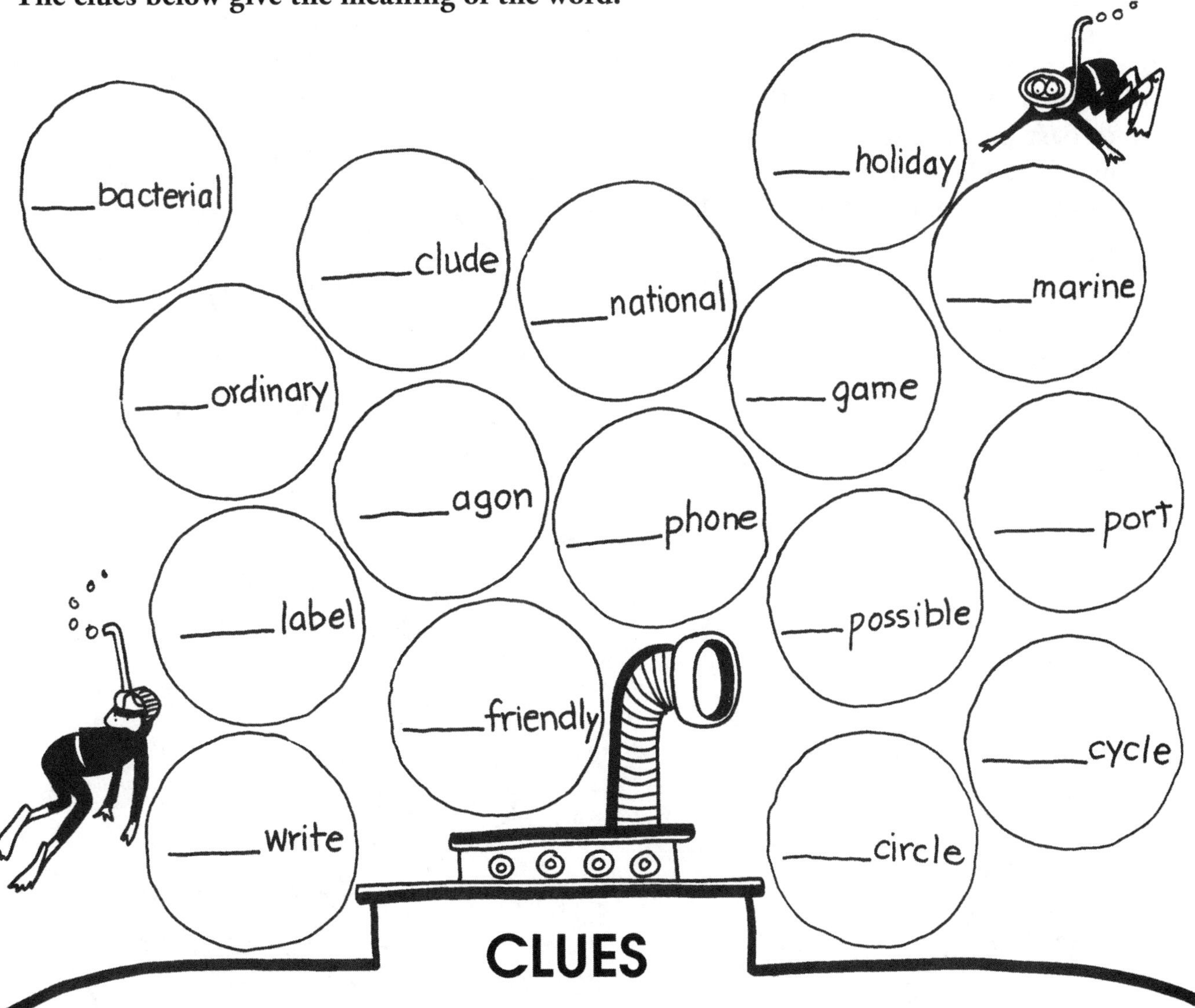

CLUES

1. under the ocean
2. a tiny phone
3. beyond the ordinary
4. to write again
5. a cycle with one wheel
6. six-sided figure
7. not possible
8. between nations
9. label something wrong
10. carry something across
11. to leave out
12. before the game
13. after the holidays
14. against bacteria
15. half of a circle
16. not friendly

Name

SURPRISING S

S is a wonderful letter. It sneaks and sizzles, spies and snoozes. Get to know some great words that show off the "s" sound!

Choose 10 of the words on the snake. Use your dictionary to check the meaning of the word.

Write the number of the word somewhere on the page. Next to the number, tell where you might find that thing, see it happening, or see something with that characteristic.

1. dissent
2. supersede
3. serene
4. suspense
5. suffice
6. cease
7. suitor
8. saber
9. scythe
10. swaddle
11. stampede
12. sincere
13. siege
14. embassy
15. essence
16. sassy
17. possessive
18. excessive
19. scaffold
20. saunter
21. swig
22. solitary
23. saffron
24. saline
25. savvy
26. cyberspace
27. sassafras
28. sieve
29. sesame
30. salsa
31. smirk
32. seize

Name

LIFE IS LIKE A SPIDER

How is life like a spider? Can you think of some ways? When you do, you are creating a metaphor. A *metaphor* is a comparison between two things that are not ordinarily compared. If a comparison uses the words *like* or *as*, it is called a *simile.*

Finish the unfinished metaphors. Try for fresh metaphors—comparisons that no one else might imagine!

1. Life is ____________________.
2. Eating snails is like ____________________.
3. The music reminds me of ____________________.
4. ____________________ (an experience) is like stepping on glass.
5. Losing a friend is as ____________ as ____________.
6. ____________ is as worrisome as ____________.
7. Being without a cell phone is like ____________.
8. When I am angry, I am like a ____________.
9. My room is as ____________ as ____________.
10. Studying for a test is ____________.
11. Poetry is ____________.
12. ____________ is like a bowl of spaghetti.
13. Homework is like ____________ because ____________.

Name

Vocabulary, Figurative Language

FACE THE MUSIC

If someone tells you it's time to *face the music*—does that mean you need to turn your head toward some tune coming from somewhere?

No, it probably means that you'll have to face the consequences of some behavior. There are plenty of phrases and expressions—called **idioms**, **adages**, or **proverbs**—that say something different from what they actually mean.

Read the sentences. Find a phrase below that helps to show the meaning of each one. Write the number before the sentence.

_____ A. I have a bone to pick with you.

_____ B. Keep your nose to the grindstone.

_____ C. Don't jump the gun!

_____ D. Strike while the iron is hot.

_____ E. Keep an eye out for the cab.

_____ F. Keep a stiff upper lip.

_____ G. Can we see eye to eye?

_____ H. He wears his heart on his sleeve.

_____ I. I survived by the skin of my teeth.

_____ J. A soft tongue can break hard bones.

1. Things said can hurt people.
2. Be patient.
3. Act brave.
4. Will we agree?
5. Watch carefully.
6. Something's wrong between us.
7. Act quickly.
8. His feelings are obvious.
9. Work hard.
10. Let's chat.
11. I got out just in time.
12. I feel pressure.

Name

DRESSED TO THE NINES!

Fred and Ginger Frog never stand still. As ballroom dance champions, they are always on the move. And, they are always "dressed to the nines"! This means they are "dressed to kill" or "really dressed up"!

These sentences do not quite say what they really mean. Write the meaning on the line below.

1. **Be a good egg.**

2. **I've got this test in the bag!**

3. **I'd go out on a limb for you.**

4. **Has the cat got your tongue?**

5. **Hold your horses!**

6. **Don't cry over spilt milk.**

7. **Blood is thicker than water.**

8. **He's in the doghouse now.**

9. **Misery loves company.**

10. **Beauty is only skin deep.**

Name

WORDS THAT STICK TOGETHER

Oops! Freddy spilled glue all over his vocabulary homework. He was supposed to match up the words that have similar meanings. But some of the match-ups are wrong.

Straighten out the mess. On each paper strip, the second word should be a synonym for the first word. If it is not, cross out the word. Then find the right word somewhere else on the page and write it on the second half of the paper.

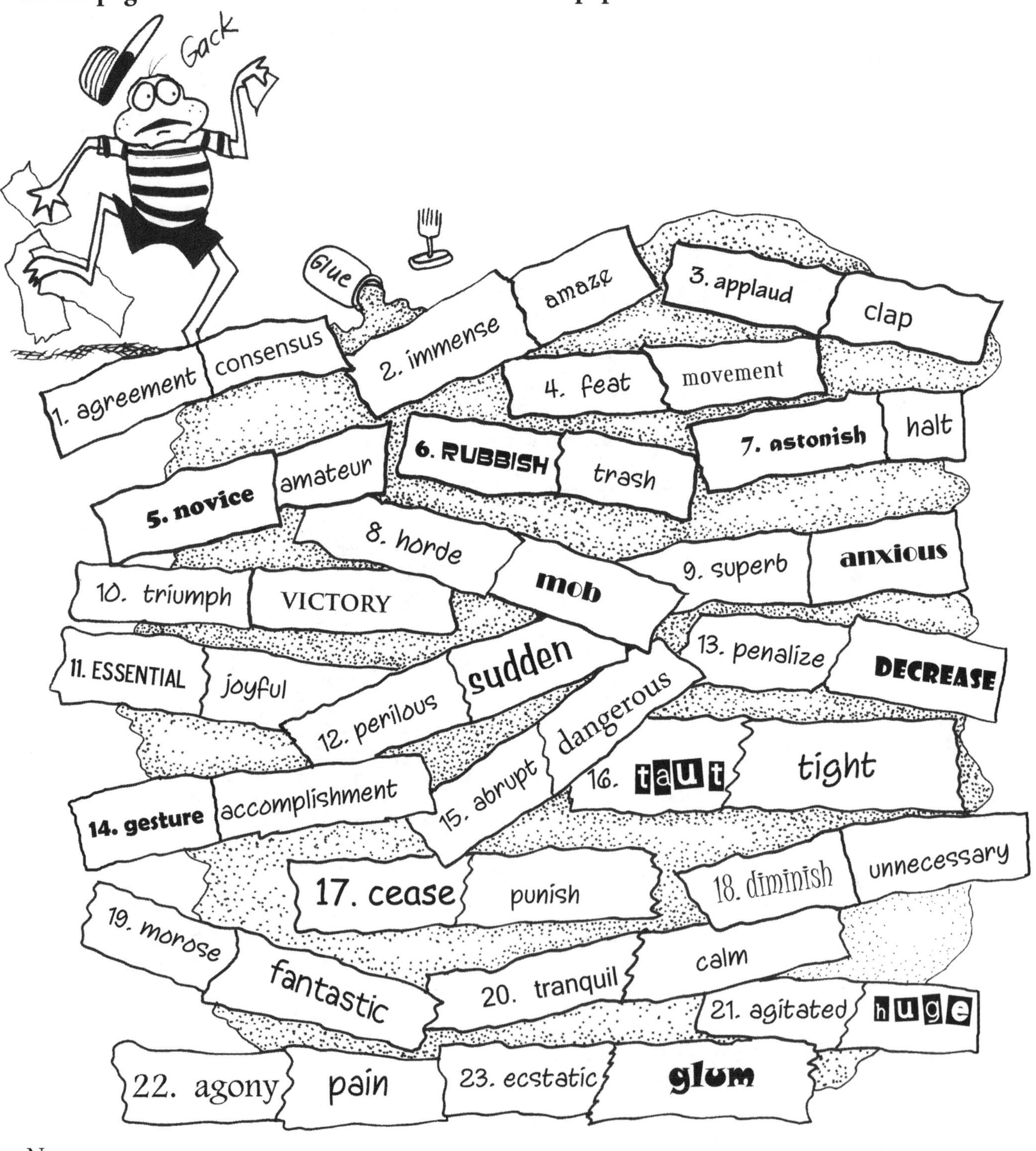

Name

A CREATURE OF OPPOSITES

Dr. Frogenstern is somewhat peeved by the peculiar creature he has created. He intended to make a creature that sputtered out synonyms. But every time Dr. Frogenstern speaks a word, the creature says something with an opposite meaning.

Read the opposites that the creature has said. What words might the doctor have spoken to get these responses? Beneath each word, write an antonym the doctor might have said.

Name

Academic Vocabulary

UNEARTHLY WORDS

When Antonia Frog blasted off in the *Amphibias 11*, she had no idea she would need a science encyclopedia or dictionary with her. Hopefully you will be able to help her with your knowledge of space science vocabulary!

Finish the puzzle with space-related words to fit the meaning clues.

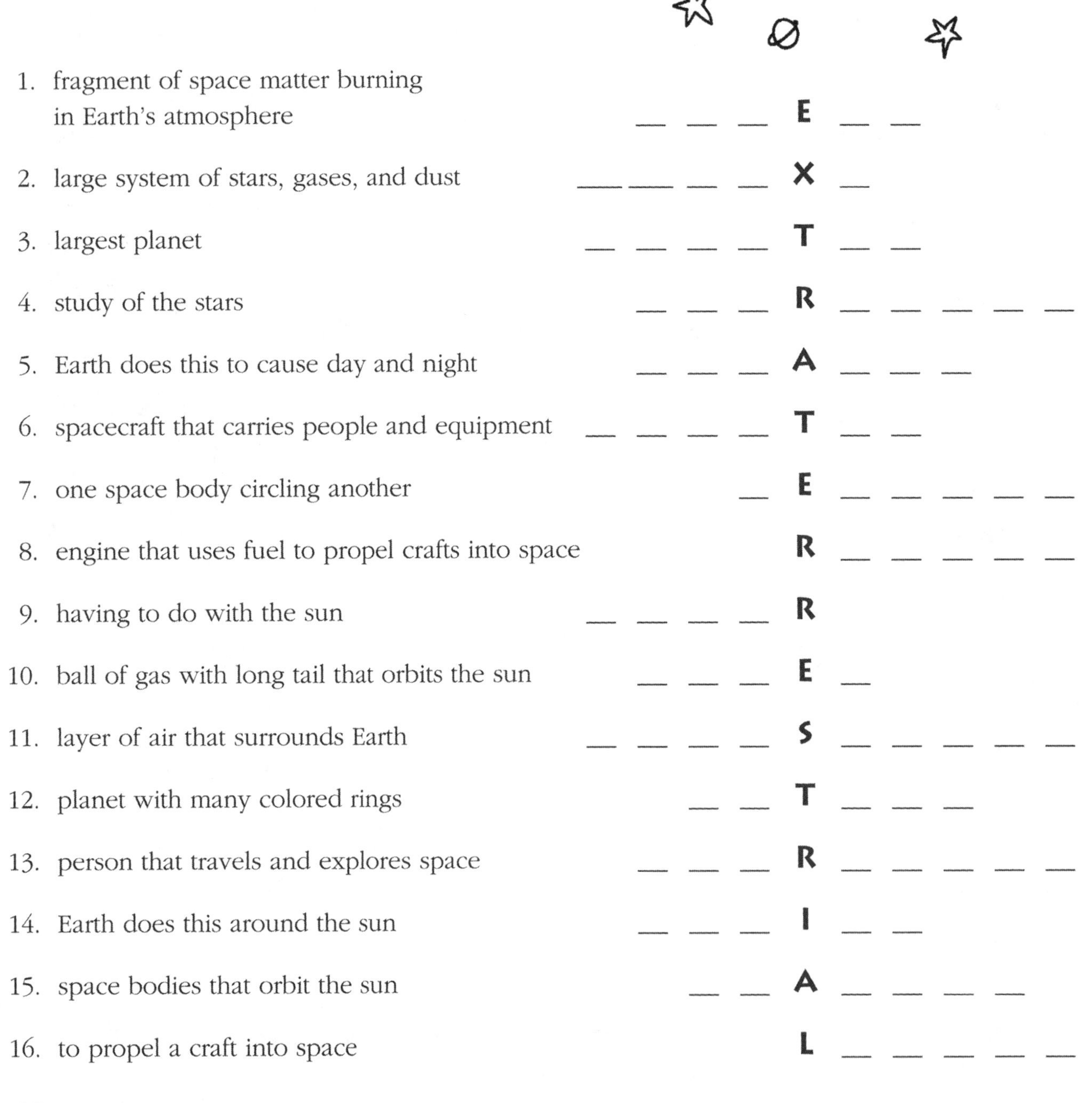

1. fragment of space matter burning in Earth's atmosphere — _ _ _ E _ _
2. large system of stars, gases, and dust — _ _ _ _ X _
3. largest planet — _ _ _ _ T _ _
4. study of the stars — _ _ _ R _ _ _ _ _
5. Earth does this to cause day and night — _ _ _ A _ _ _
6. spacecraft that carries people and equipment — _ _ _ _ T _ _
7. one space body circling another — _ E _ _ _ _ _
8. engine that uses fuel to propel crafts into space — R _ _ _ _ _
9. having to do with the sun — _ _ _ _ R
10. ball of gas with long tail that orbits the sun — _ _ _ E _
11. layer of air that surrounds Earth — _ _ _ _ S _ _ _ _ _
12. planet with many colored rings — _ _ T _ _ _
13. person that travels and explores space — _ _ _ R _ _ _ _ _
14. Earth does this around the sun — _ _ _ I _ _
15. space bodies that orbit the sun — _ _ A _ _ _ _
16. to propel a craft into space — L _ _ _ _ _

Name

ASSESSMENT & ANSWER KEYS

LANGUAGE ARTS & LITERACY ASSESSMENT

PART ONE: READING

Things Green

Green is broccoli,
Eating pickles and playing golf.
A visit to the dentist is green.
Green is the creaking of a fat bullfrog,
The smell of newly-shorn grass,
And the taste of moldy cottage cheese.
Green drips slime on a slug
And makes glue sticky.
Green is violin music and a nap in the shade.
Getting the flu is green.
Green is the feeling you get
When your best friend moves away.

1. How does the form of the passage help to communicate the main idea?

____

____

____

2. What is the meaning of the word *shorn* in the 5th line?

____

____

The Big Race

Rico and Reggie entered the Ultimate Rat Challenge. They began the race with a fast climb up and down a 2000-foot mountain of bumpy trash. Next, they paddled a raft down a rushing stream for 3 miles. Then they dove off the raft and swam upstream for 3 miles. In the next leg, they dried off and raced up and down a 30-foot flagpole ten times. Finally, they worked together to chew through a 10-inch thick rope.

At the end, they were so tired that they slept right through the award ceremony and the cheese buffet.

3. What is the point of view of this passage?

____

____

____

4. What is the main idea?

____

____

____

____

5. From the story, what can you infer about Rico and Reggie?

____

____

____

Name

Dear Felix,

I know you have planned to come next week for a nice beach vacation. I need to **alert** you to some **impending** weather troubles. The forecast tells us that *Hurricane Henry* is heading for our coast. If you did not know—a hurricane is a strong, tropical storm that gathers warm, wet air over the ocean. Some hurricanes have winds of more than 100 miles an hour. These winds cause **catastrophic** damage when they hit shore. You never know what can happen in hurricane season.

We can't be sure the hurricane will hit here in Miami, but it could. I know that you are afraid of storms. So I thought you would want to know that you might not be our only visitor next weekend. A wild visitor might be joining us, too!

Sincerely,
Cousin Eli

6. What is the author's purpose?

____

____

____

What evidence of this is given in the text?

____

____

____

7. What form did the author choose to accomplish the purpose?

____

____

How did the form help to accomplish the purpose?

____

____

____

8. What does *alert* mean in this passage?

____

____

____

9. What does *impending* mean in this passage?

____

____

____

10. What does *catastrophic* mean in this passage?

____

____

____

11. Who is the visitor that Eli mentions in the last paragraph?

____

Name

Every year, thousands of forest fires turn green forests into crackling walls of smoke and flames. Firefighters have standard methods they use to fight the fires.

In general, firefighters battle the fires first by trying to cool and contain them. They drop large amounts of chemicals and water to cool the fire. When the heat of the fire turns the water to steam, the moisture cuts down the level of oxygen in the air. This also helps to **retard** the fire.

Another **tactic** firefighters use is to burn up grass, small trees and other fuel around the edges of the big fire. It may seem **counterproductive**. But actually, it is very effective in stopping the fire—because when the fire reaches these edges, there is nothing left to burn.

Some fighters jump out of planes and parachute into the scene of a fire. They are called *smokejumpers*. These jumpers can get to the fire faster than crews that must travel on ground. They get in quickly and begin to contain the fire before the ground crews arrive.

12. What is the main idea of the passage?

____
____
____
____

13. Are fires put out faster with the help of smokejumpers?

____

What evidence from the text supports your answer?

____
____
____

14. What three things help to cool the fire?

____
____
____

15. What does *retard* mean in this passage?

____
____
____

16. What does *tactic* mean in this passage?

____
____
____

17. What does *counterproductive* mean in this passage?

____
____
____

Name _______________

18. What is the purpose of this text (including the illustration)?

____

____

____

____

____

19. Could you get to Pirate Pete's Hideout by road from Silver Point? ______________

(Tell why or why not.) ______________

____

____

20. Could the distance from Lost Caves to Cape Diamond Beach be 15 miles? ______

(Tell why or why not.) ______________

____

____

21. The note with directions is much like

a. a story
b. a poem
c. steps
d. an argument

22. Which information can be found in the text or on the map?

a. the location of the treasure
b. the size of the island
c. the height of Lookout Hill
d. the name of the cove

23. Mark an X where the treasure hunter should dig for the diamonds.

Name

On the sign, find a *synonym* for each of these words.

24. unbelievable ____________________
25. get ____________________
26. yearly ____________________
27. appropriate ____________________

On the sign, find an *antonym* for each of these words.

28. hastily ____________________
29. stop ____________________
30. permitted ____________________
31. permanently ____________________

Circle the correct meaning for each word.

32. **foresee**
    a. see four things
    b. see wrong
    c. see ahead
    d. not see

33. **heroic**
    a. one who is a hero
    b. the acts of a hero
    c. like a hero
    d. unlike a hero

34. **cooperate**
    a. operate together
    b. operate alone
    c. operate again
    d. operate before

35. **detective**
    a. the act of detecting
    b. one who detects
    c. able to be detected
    d. unable to be detected

Name

PART TWO: WRITING

1. Write a tall tale to go along with this picture. Include a good title, a catchy beginning, clear details to tell about the event, and a strong ending. Be sure to exaggerate!

(title)

Name

2. Write a short complaint about something that you dislike, something that annoys you, or something that causes you to feel angry or impatient. Make a clear point. Add some details so your reader understands clearly why this bugs you!

3. Revise this story so that it makes sense and flows smoothly.

How brave Caspian looked as he stepped into the ring! He shivered from head to his toe. His arms seemed stuck to his sides. He could not even pick up the chair that was there to protect him. He was ready to tame the lion!

The cage door opened. In stepped the lion. The lion's mouth opened. Caspian let out a terrible roar. The lion fainted.

Name

PART THREE: LANGUAGE A: Conventions

Circle the correct word or words for each sentence.

1. Rafael is the rat (who, whom) took the boat.
2. The lake is the place (when, where) he can relax.
3. He took the boat (whatever, that) did not have a leak.

4. Tomorrow he (will be, had been) boating again.
5. He'll write about this in his (dairy, diary).
6. This is a lovely day (accept, except) for the stormy clouds brewing in the sky.

Which sentence (a or b) is the best way to say the idea written in bold? Circle the letter.

7. **It is necessary for Rafael to be back for dinner.**
   a. Rafael must be back for dinner.
   b. Rafael might be back for dinner.

8. **Am I able to row in a storm?**
   a. Can I row in a storm?
   b. May I row in a storm?

Make this into a complete sentence:

9. After the boat drifted out of sight

____

____

____

____

Circle the letter that shows the best order for the phrase.

10. a. stormy, dark awful sky
    b. awful, dark, stormy sky
    c. stormy, awful, dark sky

11. a. smart, strong Chicago rat
    b. Chicago smart, strong rat
    c. strong Chicago smart rat

Circle the prepositional phrase in each sentence.

12. Is that a shark between the boat and the shore?

13. Yes, and that shark is swimming toward Rafael.

Name

14. Correct the capitalization and punctuation in this letter.

saturday august 4

dear mr and mrs Johnson

greetings to you from camp lookout your son and his cabin mates are having a great time here in wisconsin on monday through Friday the campers swim hike and sail. our french cook creates great meals. after the rainstorm yesterday campers explored new castle beach. Last tuesday july 31 they watched the movie ***ultimate camping***, and heard some spooky german ghost stories.

Today they all shouted we are having so much fun

sincerely

counselor caspian catson

I run a happy camp.

15. The juggler is juggling misspelled words. Write the words correctly!

advenshur

lafter

elephent

sircus

Suprize

dengerus

majacian

trapeeze

wiērd

enttertain

Name

PART FOUR: LANGUAGE B: Vocabulary

Circle the right word or words to answer each question.

1. LaMar is on time for the pirate contest. Is he **punctual** or **tardy**?
2. Pirates like a robust breakfast. Do they like it **tasty** or **hearty**?
3. The food is delicious. Is it **savvy** or **savory**?
4. He fancies that treasure chest of gold. Does he **want it** or **think it is frilly**?

Circle the right word for the answer.

5. Genevieve gives Georgio a smile. Would this be a **smirk** or a **sieve**?

6. The water at the beach is calm today. Is it **sincere** or **serene**?

Circle the best word for each blank.

7. It's hard to enjoy the water when a _______________ shark is circling.
   a. crafty
   b. huge
   c. menacing

8. Encountering a shark would be a(n) _______________ experience.
   a. interesting
   b. treacherous
   c. unpleasant

Write a word with a prefix that fits each meaning.

9. half a circle _______________________
10. six-sided figure _______________________
11. against war _______________________

Write a word with a suffix that fits each meaning.

12. one who sails _______________________
13. without fear _______________________

Circle one or more answers.

14. Which words have a root that means "to see"?

vision	visible	video
viable	television	vista
visit	survive	revive

Name

Write a word from the inner tube that is a *synonym* for . .

15. tranquil ____________________
16. strange ____________________
17. amateur ____________________
18. dangerous ____________________

Write a word from the inner tube that is an *antonym* for . . .

19. cowardly ____________________
20. massive ____________________
21. joyful ____________________

Circle the meaning of each idiom or other expression.

22. ***Keep a stiff upper lip.***
    a. Don't smile.
    b. Don't let your feelings show.
    c. Make a face.

23. ***Misery loves company.***
    a. When someone is miserable, he or she likes to entertain.
    b. When someone is miserable, he or she likes to have people around.
    c. When someone is miserable, he or she likes someone else to be miserable too.

24. ***Don't cry over spilt milk.***
    a. Don't cry while you are eating.
    b. Don't be upset about small things.
    c. Don't cry about a mess—clean it up instead.

25. ***I'd go out on a limb for you.***
    a. I'd do something risky for you.
    b. I'd climb a tree to rescue you.
    c. I'd lend you money even if you were not able to pay it back.

Name

ASSESSMENT ANSWER KEY

Part One: Reading

Many answers will vary. Allow any reasonable answers that student can tie to text.

1. Check to see that student answers are reasonable, and refer to specifics about the form of a poem.
2. cut
3. third person
4. The Ultimate Rat Challenge is difficult.
5. Rico and Reggie were well trained, or hard workers, or persistent or competitive; or they took their racing seriously.
6. to warn about the hurricane;
   He says "I need to alert you..." and "I know that you are afraid of storms," and "you might not be our only visitor." And he gives clear information about what a hurricane is and what damage it can do.
7. a letter;
   It was unique and captured the reader's attention; the conversation allowed the writer to warn and, at the same time, give information about hurricanes.
8. warn
9. about to happen
10. damaging, or huge, or terrible
11. Hurricane Henry
12. Firefighters have tactics to contain and cool a fire.
13. probably;
    They can get to the fires faster than ground crews. They get some work done before the ground crews arrive.
14. water, chemicals, and steam
15. slow
16. method, trick
17. opposite from what you would expect to work
18. to help someone find the spot where the treasure is buried
19. no;
    The map shows no road going between those two points.
20. no;
    The text says that the island is only 3 miles wide and 4 miles tall—so it is not possible that any two points on the island are 15 miles apart.
21. c
22. a, b, d
23. Check maps to see that the X is marked at the southern edge of Lost Caves.
24. incredible
25. acquire
26. annual
27. suitable
28. slowly
29. proceed, go
30. forbidden
31. temporarily
32. c
33. c
34. a
35. b

Part Two: Writing

1 through 3: Student writing will differ. Check all passages to see that they are clear and flow smoothly—and that they follow the directions adequately.

Part Three: Language A: Conventions

1. who
2. where
3. that
4. will be
5. diary
6. except
7. a
8. a
9. Answers will vary. Check to see that it is a complete sentence.
10. b
11. a
12. between the boat and the shore
13. toward Rafael
14. Corrected letter:

Saturday, August 4

Dear Mr. and Mrs. Simpson,

Greetings to you from Camp Lookout! Your son and his cabin mates are having a great time here in Wisconsin. On Monday through Friday, the campers swim, hike, and sail. Our French cook creates great meals. After the rainstorm yesterday, the campers explored New Castle Beach. Last Tuesday, July 31, they watched the movie *Ultimate Camping* and heard some spooky German ghost stories. Today they all shouted, "We are having so much fun!"

Sincerely,
Counselor Caspian Catson

15. adventure
    laughter
    elephant
    circus
    surprise
    dangerous
    magician
    trapeze
    weird
    entertain

Part Four: Language B: Vocabulary

1. punctual
2. hearty
3. savory
4. want it
5. smirk
6. serene
7. c
8. b
9. semicircle
10. hexagon
11. antiwar
12. sailor
13. fearless
14. vision
    visible
    video
    television
    vista
    visit
15. calm
16. bizarre
17. novice
18. perilous
19. valiant
20. tiny
21. glum
22. b
23. c
24. b
25. a

ACTIVITIES ANSWER KEY

Note: There are many cases in which answers may vary. Accept an answer if student can give a reasonable justification or details to support it, or if you can see the sense in it.

Reading: Literature (pages 22-44)

pages 22–23

1. escapades
2. soar
3. antics
4. fraternize
5. scrutinize
6. endeavor
7. venture
8. probe, comb, snoop
9. fantasy, mythical
10. great, colossal, lavish
11. culinary
12. scale
13. treacherous
14. mythical, fantasy
15. ancient
16. foreboding
17. colossal
18. lavish
19. unfathomable
20. future
21. elusive
22. legendary
23. ruins
24. bargain
25. engage
26. gander
27. remote
28. fiercest

page 24

1. ridiculous
2. thrilled
3. cave
4. reached
5. regret
6. damp
7. dangerous
8. break, rest
9. stop
10. complaining
11. upset, bothered
12. evil, scary

page 25

1. d
2. i
3. g
4. h
5. m
6. n
7. l
8. a
9. o
10. e
11. k
12. b
13. f
14. j
15. c

page 26

1. Answers will vary. Check to see that students identify four or more things specific from the text.
2. Theme identification may vary. Theme might be magic, or the possibility of magic. Check to see that student gives sound reasons or details from the text that helped decide the theme.

page 27

Main ideas may vary some. They should be along these lines:
Thursday: I am going to hunt for mermaids, and I am excited about it.
Sunday: According to legend, mermaids were women from Ireland who were sent away (banished) from earth to live in the sea.
Tuesday: Many people believe that sea serpents really exist.
Friday: I think I saw a mermaid today.

page 28

1. The Paleo-Lyths
2. Be a Little Boulder, Honey
3. I Dino If I Love You Anymore
4. You're As Cuddly As A Woolly Mammoth
5. The Cave Dudes
6. I've Cried Pebbles Over You
7. Terri Dactyl
8. The Cro-Magnon Crooners
9. The Petro Cliff Trio
10. The Hard Rock Arena
11. Tommy Shale
12. after dark
13. The Standing Stones

page 29

1. Jamie
2. Jo
3. Jeri
4. Jess
5. Jeri

page 30

1. 4, 1, 5, 2, 3
2. 2, 1, 5, 3, 4, OR 5, 1, 2, 3, 4
3. 2, 5, 4, 3, 1
4. 1, 3, 5, 2, 4, OR 1, 4, 5, 2, 3
5. 1, 5, 4, 3, 2 OR 2, 5, 4, 3, 1

Listen to summaries to see that student adequately gives orally summary of one or more limericks.

page 31

Summaries will vary. Check to see that the main points are included and that student writes in their own words.

page 32

Headlines will vary. Check to see that headlines do offer a simple summary of the news story.

page 33

Poem completions will vary. Check to see that student follows the theme of red—appealing to varying senses.

pages 34–35

Answers will vary. Look for student use of evidence from the text to support each of the answers.

page 36

Answers will vary. Check to see that student answers are based on evidence found in the picture.

page 37

Answers will vary.

1. Student should identify the difference between sentences and paragraphs in a story and shorter, individual lines in a poem.
2. and 3. Student should give evidence from the text to support the purpose identified in #2.
4. Answers will vary. Look for sound reasoning within the answer.
5. and 6. Student should give evidence from the text to support the purpose identified in #5.

pages 38–39

1. first person
2. third person
3. second person
4. third person
5. second person
6. first person

pages 40–41

Answers on all questions will vary. Check to see that student gives evidence from the text for answers.

pages 42–43

Answers on all questions will vary.
1. and 2. Student should identify differences between prose and poetry: sentences and paragraphs vs. lines, more complete information vs. more succinct ideas; poems have more imagery, etc. Check to see that student gives evidence from the text from text.
3, 4, and 5—Check to see that student gives reasoned evidence for answers.

page 44

Hold a discussion. Listen for students to give clear explanations and reasons for differences in form.

Reading: Informational Text (pages 46-68)

page 46

1. H
2. B
3. D
4. B
5. C
6. D
7. A or H
8. F
9. G
10. G
11. E
12. E
13. G
14. H

page 47

1. 1
2. 2, 3
3. poor visibility, getting too cold, difficulty controlling dogs in the wind
4. poor visibility, getting too cold, difficulty controlling dogs in the wind
5. probably good
6. cancel or postpone the race

Check to see that the text parts student circles shows evidence for their answers.

page 48

A. 40 days (step 3)
B. dries it out (step 4)
C. 20 or more (step 6)
D. organs (step 2)
E. brain (step 1)
F. putting it in 3 coffins (step 7)
G. Answers will vary. Check student explanation to see that it is substantiated by the text.

page 49

1. 4 pounds
2. no
3. carabiners
4. carabiners, tents
5. Climber's Shop
6. $59
7. 3910 Abby Lane
8. climb of Denali
9. Mountain Supply
10. Camping, Ltd.
11. 2
12. 552-9900
13. Mountain Store
14. $75
15. -60

pages 50–51

Check to see that explanations for each event match the law of motion cited.

1. Law #2
2. Law # 2
3. Law # 3
4. Law # 2
5. Law # 3
6. Law # 1

page 52

1.-4. Main ideas will vary some. They may follow along these lines:

1. In the halfpipe event, snowboarders do wild tricks on a U-shaped trench.
2. 1994 medal winner Picabo Street came back after an injury to win again in 1998.
3. Ariel skiers jump off a ramp to do tricks in the air. They are scored on different parts of their jumps.
4. Ski jumpers spread ski-tips apart to help them fly far through the air.
5. a or b

page 53

1. b
2. a
3. c

page 54

Summaries will vary. Check to see that student has captured the major ideas from each paragraph:

1. The *Titanic* was a huge, beautiful ship headed out on its first voyage. It was supposed to be unsinkable.
2. The ship struck an iceberg. People were sent to lifeboats, but there were not enough.
3. The *Titanic* broke apart and sank. Some passengers were rescued. Many were not.
4. There are mysteries about why the *Titanic* sank. The wreckage has been found, and it may help solve the mystery.

page 55

Top labels:

1. Respiration,
2. Transpiration,
3. Photosynthesis

1. Photosynthesis
2. chlorophyll
3. & 4. water and carbon dioxide
5. oxygen
6. Respiration
7. oxygen
8. & 9. water, and carbon dioxide
10. water
11. leaves
12. transpiration

page 56

A. prey
B. predator
C. habitat
D. community
E. producers, consumers
F. food chain
G. food web
H. parasite
I. Scavengers and decomposers
J. compete
K. adaptation
L. fly

page 57

Note how students share their observations about the text structure. Ask them to point out what structural components are effective, and what they accomplish. Students may mention such things as:
Bold type on featured lines, bullet points to give ideas about what the tour involves, the way information is shared about the space station, the box showing the schedule, the use of artwork, the personal contact—"You'll be so glad you did this!"

pages 58–59

Student answers will vary.
Look for ideas that are supported by the text. Students might mention that the eye witness accounts give a different perspective, add information that the detectives had not found, or add believability to the tale.

page 60

1. John Lennon's Rolls Royce
2. guitar
3. John Lennon recording
4. musical instruments and recordings and cars
5. Answers will vary. Students may point out such features as the visual organization that makes it easy to read and find information, the titles of the columns and the table, and the sequential price organization.

page 61

1. 8:21 a.m.
2. 10 minutes
3. 5 minutes or less
4. 8 minutes
5. 8:10 a.m.
6. 8:15 a.m.
7. 8:42 a.m.
8. after
9. 8:01 a.m.
10. 5 minutes
11. Answers will vary. Be sure that the explanation makes use of evidence from the text. (Students may choose the third customer, because he or she was alone in the front room from 8:30 to 8:32 while Ms. Ratskeller was busy with a phone call.

page 62

Check student maps to see that path follows prescribed route:

- From Persian Gardens south on Date Palm Avenue to the Used Camel Lot
- Across the Alley Baba to the Magic Lamp Antique Shop
- West on Serpentine Avenue and around the Mystery Spiral to the Fountain of Dreams
- Northwest from the fountain, between two palm trees across Mirage Boulevard
- Down Aladdin Alley to the back of the Oasis Juice Bar.
- Back to Mirage Boulevard and right on Desert Flower Drive
- South to Ahmed's Café.

page 63

Viva is character E.

Listen to student descriptions of how they made their decision. Listen for specific evidence from the illustration and text.

pages 64–65

Answers on all questions will vary some.

1. Opening paragraph states this. Second paragraph lists some.
2. The whole article seems to invite the public. Third paragraph, third paragraph "food and fun for everyone," fourth paragraph says so outright.
3. a variety of races and prizes, several categories, two hundred trophies, food and fun for everyone, you can bring your own slug, slugs may be given drug tests.
4. He tells about the drug tests. He says park rangers already are looking for speedy slugs.
5. long one—by the number of trophies given and the word "several" categories

page 66

Answers may vary some. Picture shows him outdoors, not in a dungeon. The dragon in the picture is not wrapped around the knight. The knight has already speared the dragon. The damsel is not chained to a pillar, she is roped to a tree. It looks as if the horse is freeing her and not the knight. The dragon is not wingless.

pages 67–68

Student notes will vary. Check to see that notes are informed by details from the two texts and possibly the illustration.

Reading: Foundational Skills (pages 70-78)

page 70

Answers may vary some.

1. one wheel
2. on shore
3. make a friend
4. below normal
5. spell wrong
6. too high a price
7. middle of the field
8. against war
9. across the Atlantic
10. on foot
11. write again
12. before dawn
13. many colors
14. not possible
15. small van
16. between states
17. not friendly
18. not honest

page 71

Answers may vary some.

perilous—full of peril
excitement—quality of being excited
frighten—make afraid
rocky—full of rocks
stormy—full of storms
nervous—full of nerves
horrific—pertaining to horror
seaward—toward the sea
hardship—state of being hard
fearful—full of fear
courageous—full of courage
survivor—one who survives
hopeless—without hope
dangerous—full of danger
sailor—one who sails
droplets—small drops
terrify—to cause terror
lostness—state of being lost
troublesome—full of trouble
heroism—act of being a hero

page 72

1. carnivore
2. zoophobia
3. fugitive
4. admonition
5. visible
6. aquatic
7. action
8. flammable
9. descend
10. dynamic
11. dormitory
12. telescope
13. transport
14. laboratory
15. arachnophobia
16. portable
17. phobophobia
18. ascend

page 73

Answers will vary. Check to see that words are real and use a root and one or more affixes.

page 74

Answers will vary. Check to see that words are real compound words.

page 75

Top answer: Title should be:
A Hole in the Pail

1. bury
2. straight
3. threw
4. caught
5. seas
6. foul
7. pail; break
8. pier; hour
9. beat
10. taught
11. buy; some
12. cents
13. feet
14. flew
15. flee

page 76

1. raise; rays
2. plane; plain
3. scene; seen
4. tale; tail
5. flee; flea
6. throne; thrown
7. toad; towed
8. Which; witch
9. steel; steal
10. Where; wear
11. write; right

page 77

1. b
2. c
3. b
4. b
5. b
6. c
7. c
8. a
9. a
10. a
11. c
12. a
13. b

page 78

1. a
2. b
3. a
4. c
5. a or b
6. b
7. a
8. a
9. c
10. a
11. c
12. b
13. a

Writing (pages 80–96)

pages 80–81

Check to see that letter has a beginning, clearly stated opinion and reasons, and a clear ending.

page 82

Check to see that written paragraph have clearly-stated argument.

page 83

Check to see that text has clear beginning, middle, and end, and that it gives information clearly and sequentially.

page 84

Check to see that writing includes sensible ingredients and equipment (all that are needed) and clear instructions in logical sequence.

page 85

Check to see that story has a clear beginning, plot, and ending and includes exaggeration.

pages 86–87

Check to see that story has a clear beginning, plot, and ending and includes correctly-written dialogue. Check to see that illustration relates to the story.

page 88

Check to see that the event is developed, and that the piece has a satisfying beginning and ending.

page 89

Check to see that writing follows the pattern and instructions for painted poems.

page 90

Check for logical questions relating to the topics.

page 91

Check to see that story has a clear beginning, plot with events, and satisfying ending.

page 92

Check the article to see that it presents coherent text that relates to the picture. Check the picture to see that it adequately represents the written article.

pages 93–94

Check page 93 for completed sentences. Check page 94 for sensible categorization and organization of ideas in preparation for writing.

page 95

Check for a clear, logical description of a character, event, or setting. Look for references to specific details from the story.

page 96

Check for statement of a main point and a logical, coherent description of evidence to support the point.

Language (pages 98–126)

page 98

1. adverb: where—links The town with where they live
2. adverb: when—links the day with they will start the tournament
3. adverb: where—links the court with they play most often
4. adverb: why—links can't understand with Flossie beat her
5. who
6. whoever
7. Whichever
8. that
9. which
10. whom
11. whose

page 99

1. correct
2. incorrect (This is not ongoing action, it is past tense.) Replace with *I was conquering* or *I will be conquering* or *I shall be conquering* or *I am conquering.*
3. incorrect—*was fighting*
4. correct
5. incorrect—*Will Felix be going*
6. incorrect—*was stopping* or *will be stopping*
7. correct
8. correct
9. incorrect—*will be burning*
10. incorrect—*Was he rescuing*
11. correct
12. correct

page 100

1. a
2. b
3. b
4. a
5. a
6. b
7. b
8. a
9. a
10. b

page 101

1. one smart two-year-old nephew
2. a rotten yellow apple
3. a round, broken toy sword
4. two small, cracked plastic bottles
5. a tiny sassy baby
6. an expensive square Chinese plate
7. a fancy red silk scarf
8. a brown leather chair
9. some terrible new screams
10. one frazzled teenage babysitter

page 102

Answers will vary. Check to be sure each phrase is a prepositional phrase, and the preposition is circled.

page 103

Revised, completed sentences will vary. Students may complete fragments in a variety of ways. Check to see that 1, 3, 5, 6, 8, 9 are complete sentences after revision.

2. There's so much silliness. These are the funniest jokes ever!
4. That's an absurd idea! Doesn't it give you the giggles?
7. All the insults are scary. They make me feel lonely.

page 104

Correct clouds to be colored:
adopt a pet
Eat your celery!
That's no excuse!
a custard pie
an inspiring story
Write in your diary.
art hanging in galleries
cute cartoons on TV
walking on crutches
I accept your present.
my red and white striped socks

page 105

1. Welcome to the Rio Grande River!
2. Drink Coca Cola!
3. Monday, September 1
4. I love French fries.
5. John F. Kennedy, Jr.
6. My favorite book is *The Thirteenth Gorilla.*
7. What's your favorite?
8. Is there really a Prince Charming?
9. Read the Declaration of Independence.
10. I'll stop at Target for some Kleenex.
11. Visit the F.B.I. in Washington, D.C.
12. Is there a Mrs. Easter Bunny?
13. Omaha Chamber of Commerce
14. Let's read the story, "Marooned."
15. I learned Spanish in Costa Rica.
16. Sir Frederick is my cousin.
17. Happy St. Patrick's Day!

page 106

1. A voice shouted, "Introducing Manifrog the Magnificent!"
2. The room went dark, for the show was about to begin.
3. A frog appeared, but only his hat was visible.
4. "Ladies and Gentlemen," he said.
5. A light flashed, and the hat exploded.
6. It rained commas, or were those quotation marks?
7. "Now I will turn these into rabbits," he announced.
8. We could not see the black rabbits, so he turned them red.
9. He asked, "Shall I turn them into doves?"
10. Manifrog waved his wand, and off flew ten doves.

page 107

Correct punctuation:
William insisted, "That window was already broken!"
"Furthermore," he said, "I was at the gym lifting weights."
Ray sweated and mumbled "I thought they were flies, not jewels."
Worst kept asking, "What bank? I didn't see any bank."
"I was never there," said Wanda.
Wanda kept saying, "I was never there!"
"I did not squeeze that ice cream man; I just hugged him," insisted Rachael.
Weekend Warrior repeated, "I was riding my bike in China."

page 108

1. business
2. twelfth
3. surprise
4. cafeteria
5. calendar
6. balloon
7. embarrass
8. license
9. memory
10. banana
11. memorize
12. necessary
13. Florida
14. restaurant
15. marshmallow
16. recognize
17. receive
18. advertisement
19. trouble
20. vegetable

page 109

1. color—3
Correct spelling for wrong words: wrinkle, tangle, shovel
2. color—3

Correct spelling for wrong words: traffic, trophy, favorite
3. color—3
Correct spelling for wrong words: omit, wallet, trapezoid
4. color—5
Correct spelling for wrong words: laziest, eastern, turkey, recognize, lemon
5. do not color—0
6. color—4
Correct spelling for wrong words: label, legal, benefit, physical

page 110

Misspelled words, with correct spelling
1. accidents
2. horses, allowed, beach
3. marshmallow, Wednesdays
4. public, lifeguard
5. notice
6. swimming, island
7. dangerous, animals
8. preservers, required
9. occupied, monsters

page 111

1. Burglar Steals Precious Paintings
2. Volcano Causes Terrible Tragedy
3. no errors
4. Zookeeper Chases Hippopotamus to Michigan
5. Magician Pulls Ninety Rabbits from Hat
6. Pelican Rescues Child from Sinking Yacht
7. Wrestler Wins Million Dollar Prize
8. Doctor Discovers Miracle Cure for Warts

page 112

Answers may vary. Allow any answer student can reasonably defend.
1. b
2. a
3. b
4. a
5. a
6. a
7. b
8. b
9. a
10. b

page 113

Answers will vary. Examine student answers for insights and reasonable explanations.

page 114

Ideas of where the language might be used will vary.
1. informal
2. formal
3. formal
4. informal
5. informal
6. formal

page 115

1. pried
2. creaky
3. wait; medal
4. throne; reigned
5. sent; chews
6. freeze; tails
7. aunt's; raise
8. overdue; week
9. hoarse
10. whoop; scent
11. cereal; Claus
12. Pedal; rung
13. fleas; hair

page 116

Definitions will vary some.
1. savor—enjoy
2. caress—lightly brush or touch, pet
3. fancy—love, like, desire
4. bland—tasteless, weak flavor
piquant—strong flavor
5. puree—a liquid blend
6. robust—full, strong
7. zest—kick, pizzazz, excitement
8. mellow—mild

page 117

1. waned—disappeared, lessened
2. noxious—poisonous, harmful
3. ghastly—scary
4. punctual—on time
5. cyclone—a whirlwind

page 118

Answers may vary some from this:
1. supernatural—above normal or above natural
2. counterattack—an attack against
3. annual—yearly
4. flammable—able to burn
5. pedestrian—one who walks or moves on foot
6. autograph—writing by oneself
7. junction—place where things join
8. decagon—figure with 10 sides
9. acrophobia—fear of heights
10. monochrome—one color
11. aquatic—having to do with water
12. cardiac—having to do with the heart

page 119

1. submarine
2. miniphone or microphone
3. extraordinary
4. rewrite
5. unicycle
6. hexagon
7. impossible
8. international
9. mislabel
10. transport
11. exclude
12. pregame
13. post-holiday
14. antibacterial
15. semicircle
16. unfriendly

page 120

Answers will vary. Discuss choices and answers with students. Give credit for any answers that show understanding of the word.

page 121

Metaphors will vary. Give students a chance to share and elaborate.

page 122

A. 6
B. 9
C. 2
D. 7
E. 5
F. 3
G. 4
H. 8
I. 11
J. 1

page 123

Answers will vary.
1. Be cooperative.
2. I am all ready for this test.
3. I'd take a risk to help you.
4. Why are you not saying anything?
5. Wait! Be patient.
6. Don't be sad or upset about something minor.
7. Connections to relatives are stronger than other connections.
8. He's in trouble.
9. People who feel awful like someone else to feel bad too.
10. Physical attractiveness does not tell what a person is really like.

page 124

1. correct
2. immense–huge
3. correct
4. feat–accomplishment
5. correct
6. correct
7. astonish–amaze
8. correct
9. superb–fantastic
10. correct
11. essential–necessary
12. perilous–dangerous
13. penalize–punish
14. gesture–movement
15. abrupt–sudden
16. correct
17. cease–halt
18. diminish–decrease
19. morose–glum
20. tranquil–calm
21. agitated–anxious
22. correct
23. ecstatic–joyful

page 125

Answers will vary: Check to see that they are all words of opposite meaning from what the monster has said. Here are some possibilities.
1. ordinary
2. friend
3. cowardly
4. cheery
5. tiny
6. please
7. praise
8. lack
9. hero
10. uncertainty
11. defeat
12. full
13. torrid, hot,
14. late
15. insult
16. sense
17. deep
18. safety

page 126

1. meteors
2. galaxy
3. Jupiter
4. astronomy
5. rotates
6. shuttle
7. revolve
8. rocket
9. solar
10. comet
11. atmosphere
12. Saturn
13. astronaut
14. orbits
15. planets
16. launch